The Big Book of

MEETING GAMES

Other titles in the Big Book of Games series:

The Big Book of Business Games by John Newstrom and Edward Scannell

The Big Book of Presentation Games by John Newstrom and Edward Scannell

The Big Book of Team Building Games by John Newstrom and Edward Scannell

The Big Book of Humorous Training Games by Doni Tamblyn and Sharyn Weiss

The Big Book of Stress Relief Games by Robert Epstein

The Big Book of Creativity Games by Robert Epstein

The Big Book of Motivation Games by Robert Epstein with Jessica Rogers

The Big Book of Icebreakers by Edie West

The Big Book of Sales Games by Peggy Carlaw and Vasudha Kathleen Deming

The Big Book of Customer Service Training Games by Peggy Carlaw and Vasudha Kathleen Deming

The Big Book of

MEETING GAMES

75 Quick, Fun Activities for Leading Creative, Energetic, Productive Meetings

Marlene Caroselli

McGraw-Hill

New York Chicago San Francisco Lisbon London
Madrid Mexico City Milan New Delhi San Juan
Seoul Singapore Sydney Toronto

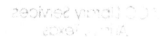

McGraw-Hill

*A Division of The **McGraw·Hill** Companies*

Copyright © 2002 by The McGraw-Hill Companies, Inc. All rights reserved. Printed in the United States of America. Except as permitted under the United States Copyright Act of 1976, no part of this publication may be reproduced or distributed in any form or by any means, or stored in a database or retrieval system, without the prior written permission of the publisher.

6 7 8 9 0 FGR/FGR 0 9 8 7 6 5

ISBN 0-07-139684-5

Library of Congress Cataloging-in-Publication Data applied for.

This is a CWL Publishing Enterprises book developed for McGraw-Hill by CWL Publishing Enterprises, Madison, Wisconsin, www.cwlpub.com. The sponsoring editor is Richard Narramore.

Printed and bound by Quebecor World Martinsburg.

McGraw-Hill books are available at special quantity discounts to use as premiums and sales promotions, or for use in corporate training programs. For more information, please write to the Director of Special Sales, McGraw-Hill, 2 Penn Plaza, New York, NY 10121. Or contact your local bookstore.

 This book is printed on recycled, acid-free paper containing a minimum of 50% recycled de-inked fiber.

Contents

Contents

Part Seven. Engaging and Energizing Meeting Participants 167
Games to add spice to the meeting recipe

Introduction

Many books have been written to explain how to lead better meetings. Rather than review the well-known principles of running a meeting, *The Big Book of Meeting Games* starts where other books leave off, by giving meeting leaders dozens of five-minute activities to use right in the middle of a meeting. Fast, focused, and fun-filled, these meeting energizers are designed to enhance creativity and productivity. The spirit of inquiry is the hallmark of these games, which help meeting leaders achieve the most common meeting objectives, such as:

- brainstorming and creative thinking

- solving problems

- reaching consensus

- ensuring everyone's opinion is heard

- making group decisions.

These games shatter the myths that surround meetings, myths of wasted time and wasted energy. They make meeting leaders and participants enablers—solvers of common meeting problems. Results, as Ford's former CEO Don Petersen once remarked, depend on relationships. The games in this book will improve the dynamics in your group. But they'll also improve the end results by:

- breaking the ice for participants who don't know each other

- engaging and energizing meeting participants

- helping meetings start and end on time.

The games guide ... and sometimes goad. They make use of many traditional facilitation and decision-making tools, such as the force field analysis and fishbone diagrams, but turn these intimidating productivity tools into quick, fun activities that can be used in any business context. These 75 games will simplify the meeting leader's job by offering a frame in which you can insert a picture of the actual meeting issue. In short, the games create an atmosphere conducive to involving problem-exploration.

Leader or Facilitator?

In some organizations, the group appoints a meeting leader. In others, a facilitator is asked to guide the group. In still others, meetings have both a leader and a facilitator. And, sometimes one person serves as both leader and facilitator. In this book we use the term "meeting leader" exclusively, a term that applies to leaders and facilitators alike.

Regardless of the foreground or background position of the person directing the meeting, the tools contained within the games allow him or her to troubleshoot, to stimulate, to explore, and to manage more efficiently the direction and ultimate output of the participants' efforts.

Regardless of the title of the person directing the meeting, this much is clear: these games will help him or her get the most out of the meeting time. They serve as molds or templates, mini-versions of productive tools that can be applied on a wider basis as time permits.

How to Use the Games

The title of each game specifies the tool or purpose of the game. Each has a subtitle as well. These subtitles are a bit more fanciful, suggesting the fun nature of the activities. The "In a Nutshell" summary provides a quick overview of the game, its purpose, and the process in which participants will engage as they "play" this game.

The "Time" element is specified next. Most of these games can be played in five minutes. A few will be even quicker and a few will take a minute or two longer. The format next specifies "What You'll Need." In this era characterized by speed and the undeniable need for simplicity, we've kept the needs to a minimum. In several of the games, token prizes are suggested (but not required) to maintain the sense of a game being played. The enumerated steps in the "What to Do" section clearly and succinctly lay out the method involved. For a few of the games, answers or possible answers are provided. And, ready-to-go handouts and transparencies are provided for a number of the games.

Finally, each game has a "Background/Applications" segment that provides valuable information, such as:

- further details regarding the origin of the tool.

- ways to expand upon the basic process.

- resources and references for additional details.

- quotations and statistics relevant to the game tool.

- relevant background material that lends solidity to the game purpose.

(Note that much of the material in the "Background/ Applications" section can be used to introduce the games. You'll find your opening remarks and transitional passages already written for you.)

To Your Good (Meeting) Health

If you've been in the workforce for any longer than a month, you're already familiar with the death traps that await participants of meetings. You, your participants, and your purpose can all be ensnared if:

- The meeting goal is not clearly articulated.

- There are no ground rules.

- There is no agenda.

- Participants are too focused on the task.

- Participants are too focused on bonhomie or socialization.

- Long-winded digressions are permitted.

- Apathy reigns.

- The agenda is followed too rigidly.

- Time is wasted.

- Full participation is not encouraged.

- A tone of intimidation characterizes the meeting.

- Discussions are repetitive rather than piggybacking.

For these and other reasons, meeting arteries are easily clogged. As a leader, you have a responsibility for both diagnosing the meeting's problems and then prescribing action that will have a salutary effect on outcomes. As Seneca noted thousands of years ago, "To wish to be well is a part of becoming well." And so *The Big Book of Meeting Games* wishes you meeting wellness.

Acknowledgments

First, I want to thank Richard Narramore, editor at McGraw-Hill, for suggesting the book and providing valuable input during its development. I also want to thank John Woods of CWL Publishing Enterprises for asking me to take this project on and Bob Magnan, also of CWL, for his editing of the manuscript that has become this book.

Part One

MAKING SURE MEETINGS START ON TIME

The first game in Part One, "Using Weighted Voting," helps participants acknowledge and appreciate the value of time. It also helps them become familiar and/or comfortable with the weighted-voting tool.

When late-arriving participants engage in the "Seeing the Big Picture" game, they're reminded of the integral nature of their presence and participation. They're also given the array of feelings that latecomers evoke in their fellow participants. The third game also invites participants to express their feelings about a lack of punctuality. To avoid preaching, participants use single words rather than whole sentences. In the final game, participants take their complaints about tardiness and convert them to positive action. (Whining without action engenders negativity.)

Starting the meeting on time sets the tone of positive perseverance that should infuse every meeting participant's every action. You can make that tone a tonic by using these games to make the most of the time the organization is investing in the participants. You can also help meetings acquire a better reputation than they've had in the past by respecting time and encouraging latecomers to do the same.

1. *Using Weighted Voting*

GROUNDING LATECOMERS

In a Nutshell

To underscore the harm caused by meeting members who chronically arrive late, this game calls for all members to list "penalties" that might be enforced. The members then assign weights to them. The game provides a chance to incorporate the highest-scoring penalty into the ground rules.

Time

5 minutes.

What You'll Need

Flip chart and marking pens; participants will need paper and pens.

What to Do

1. Begin by reviewing the negative consequences of lateness. Then explain that since the group will be meeting again, some norms have to be established. One of the most important is a policy regarding lateness. Write the problem on the flip chart and then elicit five possible solutions to the problem. List them on the chart, leaving as much space as possible between the alternatives.

2. Next, ask participants, working on their own papers, to assign a number from 1 to 5 to rate how fair each alternative is, with "1" being the least fair. When they finish, have them assign the 1-5 scores to each of the five alternatives again, rating them in terms of how likely a latecomer is to fulfill the obligation imposed by this penalty.

3. Their next step is to multiply the two weights. Then, call on each person and record his or her total for each item in the space beside the flip chart entries. The penalty with the highest total score is most likely the best to enforce.

(Note: Although the words "penalty" and "enforce" sound harsh, the associations need not be. One penalty might be that the last participant to arrive has to bring refreshments, for example, to the next meeting—preferably Krispy Kreme doughnuts or, if he or she can't afford that, a bag of potato chips at the very least. Or, nickels are contributed for each minute of lateness, with the money ultimately going to a favorite charity.)

Background/Applications

Meetings cost money. When the meeting falls into the category of a new-product launch or a conference, the costs are budgeted for and explicit. But for everyday meetings, the return on the investment of time is seldom measured. It's fairly easy to calculate: ask each meeting participant to record his or her hourly wage on a small sheet of paper. (They divide their weekly wage by 40.) Collect the papers and ask someone outside the room to total all the figures (to further protect against the possibility of identifying wages with individuals). If a meeting lasts one hour, the organization has spent that total to have these people convene. (And that's not even including the cost of benefits—insurance, payroll taxes, overhead—and time spent preparing agendas, overheads, materials, etc.)

Late-starting meetings add to these costs. According to

Michael Doyle and David Straus, authors of *How to Make Meetings Work*, the best way to deal with a latecomer is to speak to him or her privately. They advise that you not lecture, but rather ask the latecomer why he or she is late. Then, ask what could be done to make the meeting important enough so this person will arrive on time. If the answer is "nothing," you may wish to consider removing him or her from the team.

And, as the meeting leader, if you want the meeting to start on time, all you have to do is start on time.

2. Seeing the Big Picture

PUZZLED BY THE MISSING PIECE?

In a Nutshell

This game is designed to demonstrate to the latecomer how valuable his or her contribution is to the group effort. Participants write on their puzzle piece how they feel about latecomers. Then the pieces are given to the latecomer to assemble. He or she will soon realize there's a piece missing. At this point, the meeting leader explains that the latecomer is the missing piece and that without him or her the puzzle of productivity cannot be assembled.

Time

5 minutes.

What You'll Need

Prepare a simple puzzle on heavy paper stock ahead of time. Participants will need pens to write on the pieces.

What to Do

1. In advance, draw a simple puzzle on heavy stock paper, with one piece less than the number of people to attend,

6

and cut out the pieces. (If you wish, you can make a frame labeled "The Puzzle of Productivity.")

2. Take the pieces to the next meeting. Immediately distribute them, one to each participant there on time, and ask them to write down on the puzzle pieces how they feel about latecomers. They should couch their statements in the most diplomatic terms, emphasizing the positive aspects of the situation, rather than the negative. (For example, instead of "Latecomers impede our progress," the statement might read, "We need everyone's contribution. If you're not here, we can't hear from you.")

3. Quickly collect the puzzle pieces and have them ready for the latecomer's arrival. (If he or she arrives before people have finished writing, collect the pieces and finish the game at the next meeting.)

4. Begin the meeting without the latecomer. As soon as the person arrives, explain that you have a puzzle for him or her to assemble. (Turn the pieces over so the writing can't be seen.) When the latecomer realizes there's a piece missing, say, "That's right. And you are the missing piece for this team. It's hard for us to complete our project without you. But we're not going to dwell on this. Let's get right to the agenda now."

5. Segue immediately to the task at hand, to avoid embarrassing the person, but take the pieces back as you do so. When the meeting is over, give them to the latecomer and say that on the back are the feelings of the group about his or her constant lateness. Add your own positive statement about the importance of his or her punctuality.

Background/Applications

Carl Harshman and Steve Phillips, authors of *Teaming Up*, remind us that "the team's purpose should be related to, and supportive of, the overall organization's mission." Just as meeting participants sometimes overlook the importance of

functioning as an integrated whole, the group itself sometimes overlooks the relationship between the work it's doing
and how it fits into the big departmental or organizational
picture.

Just as you used the puzzle concept to illustrate the importance of full attendance, you can use it to place the meeting
purpose within the big organizational picture, to remind participants of their part in advancing the mission. A large puzzle posted in the meeting room reinforces the significance of
the group's contribution. The frame should state the meeting
purpose and each of the pieces should list a step or strategy
leading to the accomplishment of that purpose. As each part
is completed, you can color it with a bright neon marker to
show progress being made. Above the puzzle, write the
organization's mission in large letters as a visual reminder of
the importance of the group's work and the need for all
members to be present at all times unless truly serious matters prevent them from arriving on time and fully participat-
ing throughout the meeting.

3. Encouraging Prompt Starts

TIME IS OF THE S-SENSE

In a Nutshell

This game has participants working in pairs to create lists of adjectives that start with the letter "S." The words reflect their feelings about constant lateness.

Time

5 minutes.

What You'll Need

If possible, a dictionary for each meeting participant. Participants will need paper and pen. Token prizes.

What to Do

1. Have meeting participants work in pairs. If you have dictionaries, distribute them and say they can use the dictionaries if they wish as they play the game. Give them three minutes to list all the adjectives they can think of that start with the letter "S," to reflect how they feel when someone is constantly late.

2. When time is up, ask which pair has the longest list. Call on them to share it (as you eliminate any words that are

not adjectives). Then have them select two words (one for each person in the pair) and explain why they chose those particular words. (Note: If their remarks sound abrasive, temper then with supporting words. For example, if they listed "sarcastic," you might mollify the statement by saying, "It's natural that you'd be tempted to make a sarcastic remark when someone is constantly late. But it's important to hold your tongues and let me deal with the person. Otherwise, we may find conflict rearing its ugly head and then we'll lose even more time dealing with that.")

3. Award token prizes to the pair.

Background/Applications

In the words of Intel's CEO Andy Grove, "In a staff meeting, the supervisor is a leader, observer, expediter, questioner, and decision-maker. Please note that the role of lecturer is not listed. A supervisor should never use staff meetings to pontificate." His words serve as a good reminder to any person to avoid the temptation to lecture latecomers. Not only does "lecturing" waste time, it begins to erode the enthusiasm that participants may have felt when starting the first meeting.

The meeting leader plays a great many roles, in addition to those listed by Grove. As shown in this game, he or she may have to function as a traffic cop, diverting justifiably angry emotions into a detour of neutrality, turning on the red light when exchanges get out of control, and so on.

4. Converting Complaints to Positive Action

WANNABE AN AUTABE?

In a Nutshell

Meeting participants fantasize, in advance of any conflict arising about latecomers, "ought-to-be" conditions. The list is then posted in the meeting room and referred to as necessary. (For fun, and if the budget permits, have caps made with "Wannabe Autabe" printed on them and distribute to the group in appreciation of their willingness to move beyond whining to working.)

Time

5-7 minutes.

What You'll Need

Flip chart and marking pens; participants will need paper and pens.

What to Do

1. Note the words of Chinese statesman, Sun Yat-Sen: "To understand is hard. Once one understands, action is easy." Say that you'd like to achieve understanding and

even take action on a problem that frequently plagues meetings and those who attend them—the problem of late-arriving participants.

2. Ask participants to work in triads and to imagine the best possible start of a meeting: everyone's on time. Have them idealize that world by completing this prompt: "There ought to be ...." (For example, "There ought to be a rule that says latecomers have to contribute a dollar to the doughnut fund." "There ought to be a lock on the door so latecomers can't get in and disrupt us.")

3. Briefly discuss which of these ideas, if any, should be incorporated into the meeting ground rules.

Background/Applications

When quality thinking dominated American corporations, Gilbert Fuchsberg reported in *The Wall Street Journal* on the differences in the ways American and Japanese firms handled complaints. In the article, he cites a survey conducted by Ernst & Young/American Quality Foundation. In 73% of Japanese computer companies studied, complaints were important sources of new products and services. The same was true in only 26% of American computer firms.

Complaints play a vital role in focusing the attention of participants on possible trouble spots. But, if not properly guided, complaints can become a phenomenal waste of time and also lead to conflict. As the meeting leader, your role is to examine the complaints and to extract the valuable and discard the wasteful—without letting them become sources of contention or contentious behavior.

There may be complaints about latecomers or any other aspect of the meeting process. It may help you to recall from time to time the words of excellence guru Tom Peters: "If you have gone a whole week without being disobedient, you are doing yourself and your organization a disservice!"

Part Two

BREAKING THE ICE

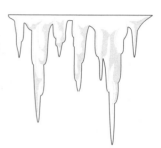

Meeting participants are social animals. And if the meeting leader doesn't provide a few moments of socializing and socialization at the beginning of the meeting (and, sometimes, in the middle of it), the participants may experience discomfort and perhaps even some degree of hostility. That hostility may be extended to the leader, to the other participants, and even to the organization itself for having required individuals to attend meetings that offer little in the way of interest, amusement, or pleasantries.

We encourage participant introductions in the first game, going beyond the boring recitation of name, department, and number of years invested. Rather, participants are asked to provide an introduction much like the ones participants on the game show *Jeopardy* give about themselves—a simple nugget of experiential gold. The nugget, though, answers the questions posed by psychologist Will Schutz regarding the makeup of a team.

The second game also goes well beyond the traditional (and usually boring) introduction. It has multiple benefits: the meeting leader learns about the capacities of the group members, participants learn about each other, and each is asked to introspect and identify the greatest contribution he or she can make to the meeting effort.

In the next game, participants advise the meeting leader and other participants of their expectations for the meeting, but they do so via a verbal voucher that expresses their commitment. Commitment to purpose is encouraged by commitment to the ground rules. The next game aids in the development of such rules by asking participants to recall their sorriest meeting experiences and then formulating a rule to ensure that such experiences are not repeated.

Business and military strategists alike know the value of metaphors. (Witness the description of the Internet as an "information highway.") Meeting leaders can also use the metaphor as an intriguing and insightful icebreaker.

The clouds of confusion that surround jargon and acronyms are cleared a bit as participants engage in the next game, "Encouraging Clear Communications." Then, when Maslow's Hierarchy of Needs is applied to meeting participants' needs, everyone benefits. Hidden needs lead to hidden agendas and the meeting leader can use this game to steer clear of both.

Creativity is encouraged with the next icebreaker, "Keeping a Meeting Log," which has participants select an icon that bespeaks their possible contribution. Vision is also called forth in the "Foreseeing Successful Meeting Outcomes" game, which has participants writing headlines. In so doing, they are strengthening the two competencies ("vision" and "external awareness") listed at the top of skills identified by the U.S. Office of Personnel Management for those serving the government in leadership positions. Finally, in the spirit of honest and open discussions, participants have an opportunity to discuss what they hate about meetings by way of a fun game that uses colors.

5. Using Will Schutz's Questions

JEOPARDIZE YOUR IDENTITY

In a Nutshell

This game capitalizes on the 30-second introductions *Jeopardy* contestants use to let the world know who they are. Each person answers two questions that initially sound sarcastic, but that are very revealing in terms of what meeting participants can "bring to the table."

Time

5 minutes (more if the meeting group is large).

What You'll Need

Flip chart and marking pens; participants will need paper and pens.

What to Do

1. Begin by explaining that teams composed of people who don't know each other well need to find out who knows what and who cares about what.

2. Ask participants the first of two questions—"Who knows?" Wait until they write down their answers, which should reveal what knowledge, skills, and abilities participants

possess in relation to the meeting purpose. (If you don't wait for them to write their thoughts, participants will simply parrot what others before them have said.)

3. Next, ask, "Who cares?" Again, wait for them to record what they care about, what they feel passionately about—in terms of the task facing the group.

4. Then ask the participants to formulate a brief introduction that sounds like the ones *Jeopardy* contestants give about themselves. For example, "I once had an opportunity to stand beside my favorite author and even have my picture taken with him." Their introductions should reveal some unique fact about them. Woven into that uniqueness should be some mention of what they know and what they care about.

Background/Applications

The questions are ones formulated by author and psychologist William Schutz, who is best known for his theory of interpersonal needs. This theory asserts that all people need—to a greater or lesser degree—inclusion, control, and being valued. You are responsible for making those attending your meeting feel included. Also, as you lead the meeting, think of ways to share the control. Assigning various tasks to various participants is but one of the ways to do this. Finally, you can show your concern for participants in any number of ways. Having coffee and bagels for a morning session is always appreciated. (Including tea shows that you realize that not all group members have the same tastes.) You can also show concern by inquiring about their activities, family, health, and interests.

Schutz's theory is often applied by meeting leaders determined to make participants feel included, in control, and valued. By asking these two questions of your meeting participants, you are including them by asking what their special interests/talents are. You are also permitting them some measure of control by suggesting they'll be able to apply their unique abilities to various aspects of the team's work. Finally, the very fact that you are asking the questions displays a concern for them as participants who have important contributions to make.

6. Learning Who Can Contribute What

PLAYING DRUCKER'S VIOLIN

In a Nutshell

Participants are asked to explore the meaning of a Peter Drucker quote and then to apply it to their own situations. The quote-application idea can be used at various times in meetings, depending on the subject at hand.

Time

5 minutes.

What You'll Need

Participants will need paper and pens.

What to Do

1. Lead a brief discussion by telling participants of the time a young manager approached Peter Drucker, the father of modern management science, and asked how he could better his management skills. Drucker advised the executive-wannabe to learn to play the violin. Discuss how such learning could enhance managerial skills.

2. Then segue to the fact that those in the meeting room have knowledge, skills, and abilities that go well beyond their job positions. Ask each person to write down something he or she does well outside of work and how it could contribute to the work facing them at this and future meetings.

3. Call on participants one at a time to share what they've written.

Background/Applications

Drucker's quotation is not as mysterious as it might initially seem. Learning to play a musical instrument teaches timing and discipline. It improves our listening ability. It exposes us to new ideas, which often spark ideas we can relate to workplace problems. Violinists know they are part of an orchestra that does not permit any soloist to dominate. The comparisons go on and on—involving the need to have a conductor, to attend to the conductor's instructions, and to read from the same sheet of music.

All of these parallels have relevance for meeting leaders and meeting participants. So does the related concept of applying other non-business skills to business problems. Leaders of high-performing meeting groups take the time to learn who knows what so tasks can be aligned with talents.

7. Determining Expectations

VERBAL VOUCHERS

In a Nutshell

You'll learn quite a bit about your meeting participants by asking them to issue a verbal voucher regarding their expectations concerning the meeting purpose. Each takes a letter of the alphabet, finds a relevant word that starts with that letter, and uses the word to introduce themselves and share their views of the meeting they're about to participate in. (You can also use this technique as an energizer later in the meeting by taking a relevant word and asking people to contribute their perspectives based on words starting with the letters that compose the relevant word.)

Time

5 minutes.

What You'll Need

Flip chart and marking pens; participants will need paper and pens.

What to Do

1. Write the meeting purpose in two or three words on the

flip chart. Use all capital letters and space them a quarter-inch apart to facilitate reading.

2. Ask participants to choose one letter from the words on the chart. They are to use that letter as the first letter of a word that's related to the meeting's purpose. They'll introduce themselves and then give their verbal voucher.

3. You may wish to use the following as an example. If the group has assembled to make a

V E N D O R   S E L E C T I O N

someone might say, "I'm Melissa from Accounting and I chose the letter 'I' for 'integrity.' I'd like to say up front that I vouch to do my best if the group agrees to employ specific criteria as we make this selection. I hope we're not voting on the basis of which vendors bring the best doughnuts or which vendors we like the most."

Background/Applications

In the contrarian words of Peter Drucker, "The human dynamics of meetings are so complex as to make them very poor tools for getting any work done." There's no denying the truth of his assertion. However, it's a truth that need not necessarily apply to your meetings.

If you have a firm grasp of the way humans relate and if you have taken the time to garner insights into meeting dynamics, you can achieve the cooperation and coordination so critical to successful meetings. One of the best ways to do this is to have participants, very early in the meeting process, declare their intentions. You need to tell participants what's expected of them and—in this era of 360-degree assessments—you also need to learn what they expect of you. What assurances or vouchers can you issue at your end? Stipulating these from the onset will save considerable time as the project approaches various milestones.

8. Developing Ground Rules

WHO'S SORRY NOW?

RSVP:
Regrets Only

In a Nutshell

The purpose of this game is to formulate ground rules. This is achieved by having participants, in round-robin fashion, express a regret associated with a meeting they've attended in the past. As they do this, a recorder captures the essence of each regret. The list is then reviewed and used to formulate ground rules.

Time

5 minutes.

What You'll Need

Flip chart and marking pens; participants will need paper and pens.

What to Do

1. Briefly lead a discussion regarding the benefit of bad experiences—they teach us what to avoid in the future. Then ask each person to reflect upon a bad meeting experience he or she has had in the past. They should consider, too, some things they themselves might regret having said or done.

2. Call on each person to give his or her name and to suc-
    cinctly share the experience (without mentioning any
    names).

3. Have the recorder write on chart paper the key words
    associated with the meeting "sin." Then convert the items
    on the list to one or more ground rules that can be used
    for the meeting(s) about to follow.

Background/Applications

Ground rules are the traffic lights on the meeting roads.
Without them, difficulties, disputes, and harmony-splitting
disagreements are more likely to occur. With them, the meeting leader need only point to the posted rules—sometimes
without having to utter a word—and participants realize
they've violated an accord to which they had pledged fidelity.
Basically, ground rules specify how the meetings will be conducted and how participants will conduct themselves. There
should be no more than 10; otherwise, the set of rules
becomes cumbersome. (It's possible, if the group likes things
streamlined, to have a single rule, such as "Treat time and
others with respect.") The rules will vary with different types
of meetings and different purposes.

As Peter Scholtes notes in *The Team Handbook*, "Sometimes a
member—usually in anger—may choose to make one of
these 'understood' behaviors a subject for open discussion."
If this occurs, the group may have to redefine or renegotiate
certain terms.

9. Using Metaphors

Hyundai or Jaguar?

In a Nutshell

Use this tool as an icebreaker with a dual purpose. It asks participants to introduce themselves through their understanding of the meeting purpose. You'll learn about them and also their perception of the task before them.

Time

5 minutes.

What You'll Need

Flip chart and marking pens; participants will need paper and pens.

What to Do

1. Introduce the game by pointing out that metaphors have been employed by business, national, and world leaders for a very long time. Cite some of the more famous ones: Peter Silas, CEO of Phillips Petroleum: "We can no longer afford to wait for the storm to pass. We must learn to work in the rain"; Winston Churchill's "Iron Curtain"; Margaret Thatcher's moniker, "The Iron Maiden" and "The

Iron Fist in a Velvet Glove"; Ronald Reagan's references to "Star Wars" and the "Evil Empire"; and so on.

2. Tell them that each will work with one other person to select a metaphorical description of the meeting purpose and their assessment of the effort required to achieve that purpose. You can present the game in either of the following ways:

   ■ Have a series of car brands listed on the flip chart: Hyundai, Jaguar, Cadillac, Honda, Explorer, etc. Ask each pair to select one car brand and explain metaphorically how and why they relate their choice to the team's purpose and the effort it'll take to achieve it. Allow a minute or two for their selection.

   ■ Ask participants to give a bit of biographical information and then explain their metaphorical choice.

Background/Applications

The business world is filled with management gurus who acknowledge the value of the simple metaphor. Says legal superstar and author Gerry Spence, "The best arguments dazzle with metaphor." Leadership authority Warren Bennis reveals in his study of outstanding leaders that many of them "had a penchant for metaphor if not for models." Poet Jose Ortega y Gasset has described the metaphor as "the most fertile power possessed by man." James Kouzes and Barry Posner, authors of *The Leadership Challenge*, speak of leaders being attentive to language: "Indeed, this attention focuses on the types of metaphors and analogies used to describe organizational problems." And business consultant Charles Thompson, author of *What a Great Idea!: Key Steps Creative People Take*, maintains, "We've always used metaphors to describe our problems and guide decisions in the workplace."

What is this simple verbal tool and how can you use it in your meetings? The metaphor is a simple comparison between two things not usually compared. It's a verbal image that enables others to grasp your point by comparing it to something else with which they are familiar. Whenever you need the comprehension and concurrence of others in order to move your plan forward, nothing works quite as well as the metaphor. You can use it in meetings by stating your goal (or some other definable concept). Then compare it to a concrete image. (Things that grow or move, games, foods, and sports work quite well.) Finally, point out how the goal or the concept is like the things to which it is being compared. Explore the similarities as a means of ensuring full understanding and commitment to the goal.

10. Encouraging Clear Communications

DIRECTED DIGRESSIONS

In a Nutshell

This introductory activity is designed to help the meeting leader ensure the meeting objective will be met. To accomplish this, one person (with a backup partner) is appointed to announce discussions that are starting to digress from the specified topic.

Time

5 minutes.

What You'll Need

Participants will need paper and pens. (Optional: a balloon on a string or a small flag or a whistle—anything the "director" can use to focus attention on his or her announcement; a token reward to be distributed at the end of the meeting if the director only had to redirect the digression five times or fewer.)

What to Do

1. Once you have reviewed the meeting objective and han-

dled introductions, announce that you are taking one further step to ensure a productive outcome: you are appointing a director who will interrupt the meeting whenever discussion is starting to digress.

2. Appoint one person to serve in this capacity. Tell the group that he or she has full authority to stand up, wave a flag (or to use any other attention-getting item), and to loudly announce, "We digress."

3. Advise the group that you appreciate their willingness to move efficiently toward desired, productive outcomes by permitting the digression-director to refocus their attention. Thank them in advance for agreeing to return to the main topic whenever the director makes them aware of their digressions.

4. At the conclusion of the meeting, thank the director for his or her role in keeping the meeting on target.

Background/Applications

One of the primary causes of wasted time in meetings is the tendency for discussions to move into irrelevant areas. Sometimes the meeting leader is involved in those discussions and may not even realize the direction in which the talk is headed. Other times, the leader may realize the discussion is unproductive but may feel uncomfortable putting a stop to it. That's where the "director" comes in—this individual is accorded full authority to move a meeting discussion back to its intended purpose.

Consider also the appointment of a time-director. His or her function is to advise the group when they have exceeded the time allocated for various items on the agenda—assuming, of course, there is an agenda and the leader has indicated how much time should be spent on each aspect of the meeting.

11. Applying Maslow's Hierarchy to Participants' Needs

BABIES, BATHROOM, AND BODY TEMPERATURE

In a Nutshell

This game is designed to break the ice by asking meeting participants which of their physical and safety needs have to be addressed before they can fully "attend" to the meeting at hand. Periodically, in this and future meetings, you should address other needs in Maslow's hierarchy.

Time

5 minutes.

What You'll Need

No materials are required for this game.

What to Do

1. Briefly review Maslow's hierarchy of needs: physical needs as the most basic level, followed by safety, social, esteem, and self-actualization. Say you know they will not be able to commit their full attention unless their basic needs are satisfied.

2. Then invite their input by saying, "So .... who needs to go to the bathroom? Who needs to know how the babysitter can reach you here? Who's too hot? Whose bottom is uncomfortable in these chairs? Let me know what you need so we can take care of those needs and then get to work!"

3. Call on each person to share his or her need, address it, and then move on to the purpose of the meeting.

Background/Applications

Psychologist Abraham Maslow devised a theory a half-century ago that has relevance even today. He believed people have common needs, which he structured on a series of levels. Basic needs must be satisfied before people can attend to the next level of needs. If a meeting leader ignores participants' basic physical needs—for example, the room is too cold for most participants—they will have a hard time paying attention to the leader's comments about purpose and timelines and expectations. Although most people are familiar with the hierarchy from *Motivation and Personality*, we'll review it briefly here to facilitate the references.

- *Physical Needs.* These pertain to the body's insistence that certain things be done to alleviate pain or simply discomfort. In meetings, you need to consider environmental conditions (Is the room too hot, too cold, too stuffy?) as well as physiological concerns (Is it time for a bathroom break? Should we get different chairs? Are refreshments needed? Does anyone need aspirin for a headache?).

- *Safety Needs.* Although some participants may be concerned about sick children at home, most will be concerned with organizational "safety" issues, such as "What happens if we don't meet our goal?" Address these concerns, whether or not they're raised. Ideally, the status of participants will not be negatively impacted, no matter what the outcome of the meeting.

■ *Social Needs.* Once physical and safety needs have been covered, you can move on to social needs, which is what icebreakers are all about. They satisfy the very basic human need to be included, to feel accepted, to develop friendship, to belong, to feel part of a cohesive whole.

■ *Esteem Needs.* Maslow identified two types of esteem needs—the satisfaction and confidence that come from competence or achievement and the attention and recognition that come from others. As participants succeed in meeting both mini- and maxi-goals within the meeting's framework, these needs will be addressed.

■ *Self-Actualization Needs.* Each of us needs to feel that we can contribute something of value, that we can make a difference in our small corner of the world. It's the meeting leader's job to help us satisfy the need to express ourselves creatively, to take on fulfilling assignments, to bring out the best that's inside each of us.

12. Keeping a Meeting Log

ICON? I CAN!

In a Nutshell

This game is the first step in keeping a log of meeting progress. Participants draw symbols or icons that represent themselves and then put them in the notebook. As the meetings progress, they will file additional information.

Time

5 minutes.

What You'll Need

A three-ring binder and three-hole-punched paper; marking pens of different colors.

What to Do

1. Ask participants to think of themselves in terms of a "self-symbol": what one object represents who he or she is as an individual? (A simple example: someone who is a technical writer might choose a pencil as a self-symbol. The person could elaborate about the eraser on the pencil and the sharp point and the length of the pencil equating with the person's longevity with the organization.)

2. Have a collection of marking pens in the center of the meeting table. Invite participants to help themselves to what they need. Distribute paper and give participants two or three minutes to think about something that represents what they do or who they are.

3. Ask if anyone wishes to share what he or she has done. Then collect the papers and keep them in the log. Tell participants that the log will be the official record of their progress.

4. If the project requires several meetings of the group, you may wish to have them do a self-symbol at the end of the project and then compare that drawing with the one from the first meeting.

Background/Applications

Relating to the world in symbolic terms is useful when you hope to elicit creative responses from your meeting members. And, in an icebreaking situation, the more creativity, the better. There'll be more than enough time for serious issues once the meeting is under way. This is especially true when issues of data-collection are needed to test assumptions.

The difference between the two types of behavior was delineated nearly 50 years ago by Alfred Korzybski when he wrote of the "Symbolic-Empirical continuum." People who behave primarily at the symbolic end of the continuum are attracted to images. They operate on the basis of assumptions and intuition rather than facts. Those who are more inclined toward evidence fall at the empirical end of the continuum. They're used to validating the information that comes to them. They want evidence, data, proof.

As a group, you need to operate at both ends of the continuum. As the meeting leader, you need to determine which operational style is appropriate for which tasks.

13. Foreseeing Successful Meeting Outcomes

IT'S A VISION THING

In a Nutshell

"Meetings" and "waste of time" are phrases usually associated with one another. However, with this game, you can set the tone for positive outcomes by asking participants what reaction their boss is likely to have if the meeting actually accomplishes something. Those reactions are written in the form of headlines, an exercise that can help develop both "vision" and "external awareness."

Time

5 minutes.

What You'll Need

Paper and marking pens for participants; masking tape.

What to Do

1. Review some of the reasons for the negativity that usually surrounds meetings. Then affirm your determination not to have this meeting waste time. Express confidence in the group's ability to accomplish the purpose within the time you've been given.

2. Ask meeting participants to project into the future. They are to imagine themselves returning to the office and telling their bosses that the meeting was highly productive. Ask them to think about what their bosses' reactions are likely to be—ranging from "I'm amazed!" to "I expected no less."

3. Have them write those reactions in the form of a headline: "Jones Faints upon Learning Meeting Achieved Its Goal" or "Smith Regards Meeting Success as a Non-Event." If they feel comfortable doing so, ask them to write their names on their banners as an informal means of silent introduction.

4. After three minutes, ask if anyone would like to share what he or she has written. (Ask any volunteers to begin by giving their name and position or department.) Then post the headlines on the wall. Refer to them periodically as the meeting progresses to illustrate a point or to commend the group for moving along or to suggest that they need to work a little harder so they can cause the Joneses in the managerial ranks to faint.

Background/Applications

The United States Office of Personnel Management has developed a list of competencies it expects those in public service to have as their careers progress from the supervisory level to the Senior Executive Service. The two highest competencies our government expects executive-level managers to demonstrate are "vision" and "external awareness." This game calls upon both as it invites participants to share in a vision of success. (Vision, after all, has been defined by 17th-century author Jonathan Swift as "the art of seeing things invisible.") When you confirm your determination to make the meeting productive, you're helping them share that vision simply by articulating it. You're looking into the future and, simultaneously, inviting participants to create that future. And, by asking them how their bosses will react when the outcome materializes as you'd predicted, you're making them aware of the world that exists outside the meeting room.

14. Learning What Participants Hate About Meetings

THE COLOR OF DEMANDS

In a Nutshell

This game has two purposes: to overcome the resistance some participants may have toward meetings in general and to learn how they're feeling in particular about the meeting they're attending. Although they reveal their feelings in a fun way—associating them with colors—they're actually exploring a serious subject—the nature of demands. The color connection could be used at different times in the meeting to learn how participants feel about other issues.

Time

5 minutes.

What You'll Need

Flip chart and marking pens; overhead projector; Transparency #1; participants will need paper and pens; two letter-size envelopes.

What to Do

1. Acknowledge that many people have negative feelings about meetings, for a variety of reasons.

2. Ask each participant to write down one sentence that expresses how he or she feels about meetings in general.

3. Ask each to select a color that comes to mind as he or she reads the sentence just written and to note that color on a separate half-sheet of paper. Collect the half-sheets and put them in an envelope marked "General."

4. Then ask them to think about this meeting in particular. What color comes to mind when they think about you as the meeting leader or when they think about the meeting purpose or the demands/expectations others have for them in terms of the mission goal? Have each write down the appropriate color on a half-sheet of paper.

5. Collect the half-sheets and put them in an envelope marked "Particular."

6. Tabulate the colors. Ask one person to tally how many half-sheets for each color are in each envelope. The recorder should write the results on the flip chart.

7. As the recorder is working, present a mini-lecture concerning psychologist Bruno Bettelheim's belief that the reason there is so much hate in this country is that we place demands on ourselves that we can't really live up to. Ask about the extent to which members dislike meetings. Ask about the extent to which dislike of meetings can be related to the demands put on meeting attenders.

8. As participants make their contributions to the discussion, ask them to introduce themselves to the group.

9. Then call upon the recorder to share the tabulation as you show the color chart on the transparency. Explain that studies have repeatedly shown that certain colors evoke certain physiological and psychological reactions.

10. Based on the color results, make a transitional statement such as "I'm glad to see a majority of blues in there. It means there's a lot of trust in this room. And ... trust me when I tell you it's time to move on to a consideration of the voting results."

Background/Applications

In an article he wrote in *Life* magazine not long after the assassination of John F. Kennedy, psychologist Bruno Bettelheim spoke about people who hate and the prevalence of such hatred. The word "hate" is bandied about so loosely that it doesn't always mean the extreme hostility to which Bettelheim referred. Nonetheless, it's important for you as meeting leader to learn what your participants think about meetings. The more honest and open their statements about things they "hate" regarding meetings, the more readily you can overcome the negative mindsets some may hold.

Getting a sense of how they feel about their current circumstances and the demands they face in those circumstances will enable you to do one of two things: either commend the group for being so positive about the task before them or assure them that some of their concerns are without foundation. As part of this assurance, you will need to tell them specifically what you'll do to ensure the concerns never develop into realities and what you'll do to transform demands into achievable challenges.

(See transparency on next page.)

The Color of Demands, In Relation to Meetings

Red = Excited about the prospects, challenges, and opportunities meetings afford

Green = Feels positive about the meeting; likely to reassure others

Blue = Calm, cool, and collected regarding meeting responsibilities

Purple = Eager to get the job done

Black = Usually a veteran meeting attender; takes a serious approach

White = Speaks mind, but in a supportive manner

Orange = Takes an optimistic view of meetings

Yellow = Prefers to proceed with caution regarding decisions

Brown = Tends to "tell it like it is" at meetings

Pastels = Worries as much about attenders' feelings as about meeting goals

Part Three

BRAINSTORMING AND CREATIVE THINKING

Old mindsets, like far-ranging roots, run deep. They can easily strangle new thoughts. We find that strangulation every single workday in comments made to employees:

- "It won't work."
- "We've already tried it."
- "Been there. Done that."
- "Just do your work. We don't pay you to think."
- "What makes you think you're smarter than our manager?"

Such innovation-inhibiting statements cause thought processes to freeze up and employees to shut up. But, meeting leaders who understand that when you don't encourage employees to make their maximum contribution to the organization, you're not getting the full value of your investment in them, invite brainstorming and creative thinking.

The games in this section incorporate a wide variety of tools, such as "Applying Autonomy of Object," which has participants personifying a problem in order to look at it from some new perspectives. The second game, "Structuring the Brainstorming Process," brings a new twist to an old method of generating ideas. The next idea-stimulator has participants looking in opposite directions in order to bring divergent thought to the problem-situation. In the fourth game, participants will examine an issue or item in terms of its inherent capacities and incapacities.

Flexibility is critical to the creative process. The fifth game, "Developing Flexibility," encourages participants to flex their mental muscles by applying numerous verbs to the problem-consideration. In a similar vein, participants use the double reverse technique to view givens from a reverse (and sometimes perverse) angle. The next game in this section helps change the pace of the meeting, through "The 'Ins' of Innovation."

Innovative thinking is developed via the eighth game, "Developing Multiple Perspectives," which has participants thinking about alternative approaches to a problem situation. The penultimate game features questions as idea-igniters. Finally, the last game in Part Three uses visuals to stimulate new thoughts.

Each of these games, directly or indirectly, is concerned with mental cross-pollination. This mixing of diverse interests, according to creativity coaches, is what creative individuals do. They let their diverse interests, curiosity, and receptivity to alternative points of view stimulate fresh concepts. As a meeting leader, it's up to you to tolerate and ultimately treasure the juxtaposition of diverse bits of knowledge. Strive to see the connections in bits of information that initially appear disparate. Help your participants to do the same. Work to draw analogies between historical facts and present practices.

Here's an illustration. Historians believe that Henry VIII died from a lack of the nutritional elements supplied by vegetables, which he refused to eat. Why? The answer might surprise you. The king believed that anything grown in the dirt was fit only for peasants. The king preferred hearty meat meals. Alas, such meals lack beta carotene—and this lack of the "dirty" vegetable vitamin is what killed the king. Could comparisons be made to certain organizational practices? Of course. And, as meeting leader you'll hold the interest of your participants as well as stimulate some lively discussions as you use the outside-the-box thinking tools (like analogies) contained in this section.

15. Applying Autonomy of Object

AUTONOMY: AW SHUCKS!

In a Nutshell

In this game, meeting participants are asked to take a concept and to personify it, to imagine it living in another time and place. From these images are born new associations. Invariably, it seems, these images lead to viable possibilities for participants and organizations alike. Albeit quick, the process yields an excellence source of innovating thought.

Time

5 minutes.

What You'll Need

Flip chart and marking pens; paper and pens for participants. (Optional: a bag of peanuts as a token "Aw, shucks!" prize.)

What to Do

1. Start this game with an example of how it works. Take a problem facing many organizations: low morale. Write "low morale" on the flip chart. Now invite participants to imagine low morale as a person, living in a different time, in a different place. Envision him as a "country bump-

kin"—the kind who really would say, "Aw, shucks," living in the Georgia countryside in the early 1900s.

2. Now ask the group to start shouting out words that come to mind when they think of bumpkins, Georgia country-side, and the early 1900s. Record as many words as you can.

3. Finally, ask the group to think of a connection between the "living problem" (low morale) and one or more of the words listed. The connection should lead to a possible solution of the problem. To illustrate: one of the words on the list might be "peanuts," which might lead to "food," which might lead to "gift certificates for good restau-rants," which might lead to an incentive program to over-come the low morale.

4. Next, take a problem that might arise (or has already aris-en) as the group meets. Follow the same procedure as in the example: turn the problem into a person living in a different time and place; generate related words; and seek connections that will lead to a possible solution. (To heighten the "drama" of the challenge, offer a token prize to the first person to produce a viable solution.)

Background/Applications

The essence of creativity is the combination of unrelated things. From the world of psychology comes an idea-generat-ing tool. Called "autonomy of object," it asks those seeking innovation to personify a given concept and then imagine it in a context removed from the existing circumstances.

The object (usually a work-related problem) is given autono-my to adapt to the circumstances in which the group has placed it. The words and actions it employs in its response to this imagined environment usually spur thoughts that would not have arisen otherwise. From these associations come possibilities for resolving the problem.

16. Structuring the Brainstorming Process

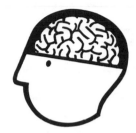

BRAIN-CIRCLING

In a Nutshell

Participants write down thoughts for two minutes, prompted by the label on a particular quadrant of a circle. After three such prompts, they examine everything they've written and, in the fourth quadrant, write assimilated ideas based on everything they've written so far. The game provides an interesting twist on the ever-popular brainstorming process.

Time

6 minutes.

What You'll Need

Flip chart and marking pens; paper and pens for participants. (Optional: two token prizes—anything circular: a bracelet, for example, or a single doughnut.)

What to Do

1. Draw a circle that takes up a whole page on the flip chart. Divide it into quadrants. Starting at the 12 o'clock posi-

tion and moving clockwise, label the quadrants as follows: Random, Purpose, People, and Solution.

2. Explain the process. Starting with "Random," participants will have one minute to write as quickly as they can any thought—any thought at all—that comes into their heads. When you call "Purpose," they have to write for another minute. This time, however, they can write only thoughts that pertain to the meeting purpose. For the next quadrant, "People," they write for one more minute, giving the names of people or groups who might be impacted by or involved with the purpose. Last, they'll pair up and, for two minutes, each pair of partners will study the words they've written in the first three quadrants of their two circles and permit the words to ignite ideas about a possible solution. They'll each write the potential solution in the final quadrant of their circle.

3. Once you've explained the process, tell them the problem about which they'll be writing. (For example, lack of a skilled workforce.) Write it on the top of the flip chart circle.

4. Then proceed with the three one-minute individual writing tasks and the two-minute paired solution-generating session.

5. Ask for a pair of volunteers to share their answers. (If you have token prizes, award their courage.)

Background/Applications

We've been using brainstorming at meetings for a half-century, ever since Alex F. Osborn, an advertising executive, described what it felt like when meeting participants were spinning out ideas fast and furiously. The rules for time-honored brainstorming include:

- All ideas are recorded, as quickly as possible.

- There is no judging of ideas until the post-brainstorming session.

- No one dominates the time by talking too much.

- People should be listening to each other's ideas and trying to piggyback upon them.

Brain-circling is a relatively new variation on this old theme. It's a more structured approach to getting those fast and furious ideas out of people's minds and onto paper for fuller and further examination.

There are further variations you can make upon this variation itself. You can do assignments longer than one minute, depending on the complexity of the problem and the length of the meeting. You can change the labels on the quadrants, depending on the issue to be resolved. And, you can have people work alone, in pairs, or in small groups for any of the quadrants.

17. Encouraging Divergent Thought

JANUS, UNCHAIN US

In a Nutshell

Working in pairs, meeting participants will consider an issue from an opposing point of view and come up with a possible resolution. The purpose of the game is to yield fresh insights via opposites.

Time

5 minutes.

What You'll Need

Handout; participants will need paper and pens. (Optional: promotional literature from the Janus financial services firm, to be obtained in advance.)

What to Do

1. Explain who Janus was and why a type of thinking has been named after him. To show how this thinking can unchain us from the manacles of dull thoughts, give the following two examples:
   - The writers who created *Columbo* violated mystery-writing tradition; instead of revealing the murderer only

at the end of the story, they revealed the murderer within the first few minutes.

- A property management firm invited cab drivers to its unveiling of a new, upscale shopping mall in New York City.

2. Assign a relevant problem to the group, one with which they've been grappling or may have to grapple in the future. Distribute the handout (page 52), which has specific pairs of opposites to stimulate solutions. Encourage them to tackle as many pairs as they can during the allotted time of four minutes.

3. Ask for a volunteer to share an answer he or she came up with. (Optional: Invite a neutral third party in to listen to the ideas. He or she will select the most viable and award the winners the promotional literature.)

Background/Applications

Janus was an ancient god whose dual profile was found on Roman coins. One profile looked back at the year just ending and the other faced forward, looking toward the year about to begin. (The month of January is named after Janus.)

Lao-tzu, the Chinese philosopher, asserted, "All behavior consists of opposites. Learn to see things backward, inside out, and upside down." When we insist on seeing things as we've always seen them, we shackle ourselves to hackneyed ideas. It's only by breaking the chains of tradition and forging new ones that we can move beyond the past, beyond the present, and into the future.

The greater the level of diversity—in individuals *and* in their ways of thinking—the greater the number of ideas and the number of usable ideas. Remember the advice of Tom Peters: "Hire a few genuine off-the-wall sorts—i.e., collect weirdos. In addition to seeking curious people in general, try to implant a few real head cases into your joint from time to time."

Janusian Opposites

Young	Old
Safe	Dangerous
Individual	Organizational
Partial	Whole
Loss	Gain
Trust	Suspicion
New	Unfamiliar
Clarity	Confusion
Risky	Guaranteed
Public	Private
Tears	Laughter
Profit	Loss
Full	Empty
Quick	Slow

18. Specifying Capability and Incapability

CAN 'N' CAN'T

In a Nutshell

Paralleling the concept of opposites, this game has participants think of things not associated with a particular object. These new perspectives often lead to new solutions. The game truly stimulates innovative thinking.

Time

6 minutes.

What You'll Need

Handout #1; participants will need paper and pens.
(Optional: a set of coat hangers as a token prize for the winning triad.)

What to Do

1. Explain that the game involves a simulation. A local manufacturer of wire coat hangers is going out of business. He has donated a truckload of new coat hangers to your firm. The group is meeting to determine what to do with them.

2. Distribute the handout (page 56) to pairs and encourage them to come up with ideas by considering what *can't* typically be done with a coat hanger.

3. Allow three minutes for this brainstorming. (Optional: Offer a prize to the pair with the longest list of ideas or the best idea, as determined by an appointed panel of judges. Choose one pair to serve as judges. Emphasize objectivity: "Of course, you wouldn't choose your own just because it's your own.")

4. Take a work-related problem and, for the remaining two minutes, consider what can and can't be done with it.

Possible Answers

■ Can't wear it, but you could make jewelry out of it.

■ Can't admire it aesthethically, but you could make wire sculptures from it.

■ Can't eat it, but you could use it in the garden as a tomato stake.

■ Can't shoot with it, but you could use it as a weapon and keep it in your car.

■ Can't put it in your pocket, but you could make a belt out of it.

■ Can't hang them from the ceiling, but you could shape them into feet and let stocking manufacturers display their wares in department stores.

Background/Applications

One of the hallmarks of creativity is the ability to find new uses for old things. In *The Art of Thinking*, Vincent Ruggiero maintains we can always find new uses for old things. Given the waste-disposal problems we face in this nation, such thinking is required. He cites as examples a barber in St. Louis who combines hair clippings with peat to form a rich potting soil to revitalize the arid soil in parts of the Third

World and the college student who used empty beer cans as window curtains.

Recycling efforts are part of many environmentally conscious companies. Can 'n' Can't Thinking helps develop that consciousness. Beyond recycling, though, the tool can be applied to areas needing improvement—areas such as customer service, process improvement, communications, etc.

Hanger Hang-ups

Directions: Get free from your stale thinking about hangers. Don't be "hung up" by traditional ideas of what a hanger can do or is designed to do. Instead, look at all the things a hanger can't do and let those ideas lead you to new possibilities for hangers. One example is provided.

Can't	*But You Could*
Can't eat it	Eat *with* it: use as marshmallow sticks for campers

19. Developing Flexibility

FLEX THOSE MENTAL MUSCLES

In a Nutshell

This game affords practice with mind flexing. Working in triads, participants first determine a problem facing them and then analyze the problem by being flexible in their thinking.

Time

5 minutes.

What You'll Need

Handout #1; Flip chart and marking pens; participants will need paper and pens. (Optional: three pieces of taffy for the winning triad.)

What to Do

1. Define "mind flexing": the process of viewing a situation from multiple new perspectives. These new perspectives are created via action-oriented verbs, such as "bend."

2. Then share this example. Many employees are reluctant to change, sometimes for very valid reasons. If you look at this reluctance and "fragment" it, you might be able to overcome it with a program of incremental changes. In

other words, you could schedule the introduction of some aspect of the change over a given period, helping employees get used to the new order of things a little at a time, rather than all at once.

3. Have the participants form triads. Distribute the handout (page 59) to each triad. Have them work on the other flex possibilities. After three minutes, ask one person from each triad to share what they've done. (Optional: Collect the papers and have someone deliver them to a member of senior management known for innovative thinking— someone you've contacted earlier—who will determine which ideas are the most flexible/creative. Award the taffy pieces to the winners in honor of their flexibility.)

Background/Applications

"Outside-the-box" thinking is a term so popularized that businesspeople are beginning to tire of hearing it. Nonetheless, such thinking is vital because, as that truism goes, "If you always do what you've always done, you'll always get what you've always got." It's normal and natural to veer toward the familiar, the known, the tried and true. But the normal and natural lead to negative consequences: us-versus-them thinking, groupthinking, stereotyping, finger-pointing, resistance to change.

Brand-new ideas help meeting participants avoid these pitfalls. So, if you're seeking truly original thought, you need to move the members of your group in directions they've never gone before. You need to encourage mind flexing.

It's not easy, for we cling to our beliefs, attitudes, our way of looking at the world. But the world is changing so rapidly that innovative thought is at a premium. Perhaps the best rationale for adaptability is found in the bumper stickers that read, "Adapt or Die!" And the best rationale for flexibility may very well be this observation by Einstein: "The problems that exist in the world today cannot be solved by the level of thinking that created them."

Situations Needing Improvement

Directions: It helps to be flexible in your thinking when looking at a situation that needs improvement. Several such work-related situations are listed below. You're also free to consider an actual situation you'd like to see improved where you work. With your partners, discuss possible improvements in light of the verb suggestions supplied.

No benchmarking going on

Secretaries not given challenging assignments

Time wasted in socializing

Bosses who micromanage

Other: _____

Now select one of the following verbs and apply it to any one of the problems above. Expand your thinking and let the new verb ideas lead to a possible solution.

- Bend it

- Break it

- Exaggerate it

- Associate it

- Analogize it (make an analogy)

- State the knowns of it

- Consider the ideals

- Minimize it

- Maximize it

20. Applying the Double Reverse Technique

NURSE THE REVERSE

In a Nutshell

The tool used in this game is the double reverse technique. It asks meeting participants to provide reverse questions to a problem they're facing. Then they go in reverse again, supplying answers to the reverse questions. From those answers, opposite ideas often emerge, creatively leading to a workable solution.

Time

6 minutes.

What You'll Need

Colored adhesive circles, one inch in diameter; masking tape; participants will need paper and pens. (Optional: token prize, such as the leftover adhesive circles.)

What to Do

1. Explain how the reverse process works. By asking reverse questions to encourage divergent thought, participants can often reverse their thinking a second time and wind

up with creative replies that contribute to resolving the problem.

2. Form triads. Assign the problem—one that meeting participants need to solve. Then, ask them to take two minutes to form reverse questions, such as the following:
   - How could we make this more expensive?
   - How could we make this plan fail?
   - How could we make upper management hate it?
   - How could we make it more complicated?
   - How could we make others doubt it?
   - How could we make morale worse?

3. Have the triads exchange questions. For the final two minutes, have them answer one question and then ask the opposite question for the answer. From that, a solution will emerge. (For example, for the question "How could we make it more expensive?" an answer might be "By asking everyone in the organization for an opinion." The reverse of that question might be "How can we limit the input?" And the answer to that might be "Gain approval from key decision-makers.")

4. Ask one person in each triad to post the triad answer on the wall. Give three adhesive circles to each triad. Then have each person use his or her circle to cast a vote for one of the wall postings. The triad that garners the most votes wins the token prize.

Background/Applications

As creativity guru Charles Thompson, author of *What a Great Idea! Key Steps Creative People Take*, points out, such reversals are not new. Every time we play the role of devil's advocate, we're challenging the existing order. He cites the example of a pamphlet issued by the U.S. Environmental Protection Agency as part of an awareness campaign. Titled "How to Destroy the Earth," it contains tips like these:

- Leave the lights on.

- Photocopy everything.

- Buy over-packaged products.

- Ask for plastic supermarket bags.

- Drive everywhere. (Don't walk, bike, or take public transportation.)

- Reach for paper towels. (Why use one made of cloth?)

- Pour used motor oil into the ground.

- Mow your lawn daily.

- Throw leaves out with the trash.

- Put off that tune-up. ("If only 100,000 car owners followed this simple tip, we'd add 90,000,000 pounds of greenhouse gases to the air.")

The agency used opposites as well to explain the pamphlet's purpose: "You can *save* the earth by knowing what you are doing to *destroy* it" (italics added).

This tongue-in-cheek approach can be used at several stages of the meeting; it invites perspectives that might not otherwise be brought to a topic or a problem.

21. Changing the Pace of the Meeting

THE "INS" OF INNOVATION

In a Nutshell

The purpose of this game is to stimulate creativity by switching the pace and tone of the meeting. Participants make lists of words starting with the letters "in." These words are then applied to the meeting situation or problem that needs some new insights.

Time

6 minutes.

What You'll Need

Flip chart and marking pens; participants will need paper and pens. (Optional: a token prize that begins with the letters "in," such as a drawing **in**strument.)

What to Do

1. This stop-the-action game is best used when you need a change of pace. If you sense trouble brewing, for example—tension among the meeting participants or frustration because of a stalemate—don't allow it to foment.

Instead, say, "I think we need to take our minds off our troubles now and have some fun by thinking creatively."

2. Ask participants to take three minutes to write down as many words as they can that start with "in" and that relate to the meeting process, purpose, or problem.

3. Award a token prize to the person with the longest list. Then ask him or her to select one word from the list and briefly explain its relationship to the meeting.

4. For the final minute, segue back to the point at which you'd left off with a statement like this: "The fact that we can get emotional or even bogged down with this issue demonstrates that we care about it. However, as your meeting leader, I need to channel what you're feeling into the best possible direction. Your 'in' ideas have given us some new possibilities. Frank, continue with what you were saying now. As you do so, however, try to think of ways—ideally '**in**-ways'—that we can jump this hurdle." (If possible, incorporate one of the "in" words from their lists into your segue.)

Possible Answers

invent
influence
intent
inception
incentive
incident
inclusion
inclination
increase
incubation
indulgence
independence
information
industry
initiative
informality

Background/Applications

In *Verbal Judo*, George Thompson compares handling anger the way a martial artist handles force: gently. (In fact, the word "judo" means "the gentle way.") As a meeting leader who must contend with occasional emotional flare-ups or the frustration that can cause them, you can use the wisdom of the martial artists to divert the tension caused by conflict and frustration. Thompson speaks of refusing to counteract an opponent's approach, refusing to hammer back at him or her. Rather, he suggests moving with the person, challenging their momentum, causing them to lose their balance. As he says, your efforts should be "redirective" and not confrontational.

When you use games like "The 'Ins' of Innovation" with their change-of-direction approach, that's exactly what you're doing. You're temporarily diverting the emotions of one person or several, engaging them in an entirely different activity. Ideally, by the time you turn to that person again, he or she will be less obstructive and more willing to discuss the issue. Along the way, ideally, some new ideas will have emerged.

22. Developing Multiple Perspectives

OH, BABY!

In a Nutshell

This fun game encourages the diplomacy and respect that help meetings flow smoothly. It also helps develop creative perspectives. Basically, meeting participants look at ugly baby pictures (belonging to the meeting leader and his or her family members) and find diplomatic ways to express their comments. They'll have to find aspects other than ugliness to comment on, thus forcing them to look beyond the obvious.

Time

5 minutes.

What You'll Need

One ugly-baby picture of you or family members for each participant; participants will need paper and pens.

What to Do

1. Begin with the observation that the essence of creativity is looking at what everyone else is looking at and seeing something no one else sees. Then say you'd like them to look at a photograph and write a comment that is not

negative but also not hypocritical. It must be expressed truthfully but diplomatically.

2. Distribute the photographs and allow three minutes for participants to write their comments.

3. For the remaining two minutes, ask for a volunteer to share his or her comment.

4. Conclude by asking participants to keep this same open-minded approach to the issues they'll have to resolve and the problems they'll have to solve as the meeting progresses.

Background/Applications

Perhaps the best example of the need to remain open regarding what you've learned and what you have yet to learn comes from this interesting anecdote. When Einstein was on the faculty at Princeton University, social events were held so that students and professors could mingle. The story goes that a bright-eyed undergraduate approached the genius but apparently failed to recognize him.

The student introduced himself and then politely asked, "And what do you do here?"

"Young man," Einstein is reported to have declared, "I have devoted my life to the study of physics." The student's eyes grew round with wonder and confusion.

"Really?" he exclaimed. "I finished physics in one semester!"

Exercises that force us to strip away preconceptions and find something deeper or more meaningful or new in what we're viewing are valuable exercises indeed. Continue to look for ways to challenge stereotypic thinking. And, in the course of your meetings, make certain you've appointed a recorder. It's all too easy, especially with a high-energy group, for ideas to get lost.

23. Using Questions to Stimulate Ideas

IDEA-IGNITERS

In a Nutshell

The purpose of this game is to quickly generate new ideas in response to questions. Whenever you find, in your duties as meeting leader, that participants need a mental battery boost, show the transparency list of questions and stimulate the growth of original thoughts.

Time

5 minutes.

What You'll Need

Overhead projector; Transparency #1; flip chart and marking pens; participants will need paper and pens. (Note: If you prefer, a different set of questions can be asked on the transparency.)

What to Do

1. Take an issue with which participants are currently grappling. Write it on the flip chart so it's clearly and quickly visible to everyone in attendance.

2. Show Transparency (page 70) and ask participants to write down answers to the questions listed, in relation to the problem on the flip chart.

3. After two minutes, call on a few participants (or ask for volunteers) to share their answers for discussion.

Background/Applications

Never underestimate the power of questions to set a course of action, to motivate a meeting group, to validate purpose, and to help participants avoid mistakes. For the meeting leader committed to maximizing the time and effort, questions are the perfect tool. Their range extends from the simple (as shown on the transparency) to the complex. They have multiple functions and provide multiple benefits.

But as issues grow more complex, so does the framing of the questions. As an example, if you ask the typical adult, "How do you get to heaven?" the answers will be strikingly similar: "Do good deeds" or "Follow the Golden Rule." If you ask a child, not yet encrusted by hackneyed literalism, the answer might be "You have to take the God elevator."

But if you ask the adults the question in a different fashion, the answer might be more creative. Unfortunately, in these turbulent times, we ask and answer questions quickly. (As Norman Mailer wryly notes, "There's this faculty in the human mind that hates any questions that takes more than ten seconds to answer.") Consequently we often fail to frame questions and answers in a format that will elicit the reactions we hope to receive.

IDEA IGNITERS

New? Blue? Askew? Knew? Pursue?

Renew? Grew? Due? Misconstrue? Outdo?

Clue? Clue? Too? View? Flew?

Few? Taboo? Threw? Revenue? Glue?

Rue? True? Through? Crew? Retinue?

Sue? Imbue? Debut? Ensue? Knew?

Unscrew? Review? Pursue? Undo? Renew?

24. Employing Visual Stimuli

A PICTURE CAN SPARK 1000 WORDS

In a Nutshell

This idea-sparker asks participants to view random, colorful, interesting visual images and to let ideas emerge through free association. Use these thought-provocative *visuals* as an alternative to thought-provocative *questions* to inspire creativity and brainstorming.

Time

5 minutes.

What You'll Need

A stack of ads and photos taken from a variety of old magazines; flip chart and marking pens; participants will need paper and pens.

What to Do

1. Initiate the exercise by commenting on how a single image, yes, is sometimes worth a thousand words, but can also evoke a thousand words in response. Some of these words are internal dialogs (e.g., the photo of the fireman carrying a child in his arms in Oklahoma City).

Others are commentaries and discussions that would never have been spawned if not for the visual stimulus.

2. Write on the flip chart a meeting issue for which creative thinking is needed.

3. Ask participants to take a bunch of the magazine ads and photos and flip through them, glancing at the meeting issue from time to time as they do so. They should record quickly—in phrases, not sentences—whatever half-formed ideas randomly jump out at them as possible directions in which to take the issue.

4. After two minutes, call on each person to share one possibility prompted by the ads and photos.

Background/Applications

Visualization is a technique used by athletes, goal-setters, and seriously ill patients alike. It calls upon imagination, which Einstein believed to be more important than knowledge. (In fact, management guru Tom Peters asserts that imagination is the only source of true value in the new economy.) Einstein also acknowledged, "When I examined myself, and my methods of thought, I came to the conclusion that the gift of fantasy has meant more to me than my talent for absorbing positive knowledge."

It's perfectly acceptable to think weird or bizarre or fanciful thoughts once in a while. After all, it's much easier to tame a wild idea than to breathe life into a dull one.

Encourage the crazy ideas. Accept them willingly into the cadre of considered thoughts. Allow some time for playfulness in the meeting, for upsetting the established order, for shifting the paradigms. Certitude is fine for catechism but can be deadly for creativity. Use visual and verbal stimulation to bring forth bright ideas.

Part Four

GAMES TO SOLVE PROBLEMS

The meeting-leader has numerous opportunities to establish a problem-solving mindset for the group and thus create a climate in which creative problem-solving can occur and even flourish. The games that follow will assist you in various aspects of the problem-solving process:

- Find information (preferably through data-collection) and define the problem.

- Generate several possible solutions.

- Choose a solution.

- Implement it.

- Gather data to compare the pre-solution status with the post-solution status.

- Evaluate the results.

- Make adjustments as needed.

- Widen and deepen the scope of the solution.

The first game in this section helps participants obtain clarity on the definition of the problem. The second game, "Using the Is/Is Not Analysis," although presented here as a way to deal with the problem of a brewing conflict, can be used on the problem that is the focus of the meeting. It's a form of problem-definition that delineates what a given thing is but also what it isn't. By specifying such considerations, you can move the group from the level of (sometimes erroneous) facts and opinion to the level of mission importance.

Similarly, the matrix diagram in the third game widens the lens through which the problem is being viewed so that participants can subsequently zoom in on the specific problem they need to address. And, in keeping with the belief that a problem well-defined is a problem half-solved, the five-why technique is presented in the fourth game as a means of determining root cause.

The fifth game uses a classic quality tool, the fishbone diagram, and demonstrates multiple approaches for working with the relationship between cause and effects. Another classic, Lewin's force field analysis, is the sixth game, which requires considerable interaction among meeting participants. Next comes storyboarding, a means of examining the component aspects of a given problem situation.

The focus of the eighth game is eliciting improvement ideas, many of which can be pulled from participants' heads within minutes—if the right conditions have been established. The next game, "Using a Multi-Pronged Approach," addresses the importance of using diversity of thought, illustrating the point via a tricky brainteaser. The tenth game has participants viewing "problems" as "opportunities." Such a perspective can help keep participants from becoming discouraged from the onset of their task.

The next game develops appreciation for differences in thinking styles, stressing the importance of both convergent and divergent thought in problem-solving. "Exploring Problems from a Different Viewpoint" is the title of the twelfth game; its subtitle is "Mother Nature Saves Father Time." In it, game-players are asked to view problems from a perspective they seldom or never use, much as Jonas Salk did when he discovered the polio vaccine.

In the next game you'll have participants testing their assumptions; it serves as a reminder that data are more valuable than opinions. Finally, the correlation chart is presented as a tool for gathering and analyzing data prior to finding solutions for the problems being explored.

25. Obtaining Clarity on Problem-Definition

Ask Your Local Druggist

In a Nutshell

It's been said that a problem well-defined is a problem half-solved. Participants will define the problem in their own words as you record their statements on the flip chart. Then you'll iron out the verbal wrinkles so participants will have a tightly woven fabric of understanding regarding the problem they're facing.

Time

7 minutes.

What You'll Need

Flip chart and marking pens; participants will need paper and pens.

What to Do

1. Begin with this hypothetical example. "Assume we're meeting as a task force to make recommendations about the potential drug problem in the workplace."

2. Call on each person to define what is meant by the "drug problem." The first person cannot use the word "drug" or "drugs." The second person cannot use "drug" or "drugs" or any other drug-related word that was used by the first person ("substance abuse," for example). The third person cannot use any of the defining terms used by those who preceded him or her. Finally, have the fourth person define "drug problem" without using any of the terms used by the preceding three.

3. Explain that people in a meeting often have different opinions of what the problem is that they've been assembled to solve.

4. Ask each person to write down what he or she believes they are supposed to do before the meeting is over to solve the problem. Allow three minutes or so. Then, record their answers on the flip chart.

5. Bring closure to the exercise by commenting upon the different ways they have defined the problem.

Background/Applications

The progress to be made following problem-definition can be likened to the S-curve, a graph that shows the connection between the effort required to learn at the beginning of the learning process and the success that results from expended effort.

The initial stages of learning can be laborious. Think about the effort it took to learn to print your first name when you were in kindergarten. Compare that effort with the speed with which you can print or type your name now. If you know shorthand, you might be able to write more than 100 words a minute, but in the beginning you could probably produce only one word a minute.

The plotting of the two variables, "Results" and "Effort," usually produces a line that resembles an elongated "S." The flat bottom of the letter shows that much effort can initially go in without much upward movement toward progress. Then, at some point, the results come much more readily. Similarly, defining the problem may not produce much in the beginning. But once everyone is fully informed and in agreement about the nature of the problem, the group will more quickly make progress toward a resolution.

26. Using the Is/Is Not Analysis

Is It Not?

In a Nutshell

Working in pairs, participants list all the things a meeting is not. Such listing helps focus their attention on the true meeting purpose.

Time

5-7 minutes.

What You'll Need

Participants will need paper and pens. (Optional: token prize, such as a bunch of grapes labeled "Is Not Sour.")

What to Do

1. You can interrupt the potential flow of conflict and divert the stream of angry words likely to come. When you sense tension brewing, ask participants to form pairs and to write as fast as they can for three minutes to record what a meeting is not. It is not, for example, a "gripe session."

2. Determine which pair has the longest list, ask the two to read it, and award them a token prize.

3. Segue back to the discussion at hand by making a verbal transition such as this: "Thank you for reminding us of our purpose here. If any of you have strong opinions, you know we want to hear them. What we don't want are opinions expressed in such a way that they offend others or destroy the cooperation we've managed to display so far. Now, where were we?" (Or, "Joan, you were saying....")

Possible Answers

- Is not a gripe session.

- Is not a one-person show.

- Is not an emotional circus.

- Is not a way to get out of work.

- Is not an automatic waste of time.

- Is not a battlefield.

- Is not a social hour.

Background/Applications

Charles H. Kepner and Benjamin B. Tregoe developed a deceptively simple way to solve problems. Called an "is/is not analysis," the process requires problem-solvers to determine where a given problem does and where it does not occur or to determine what the situation is and what it is not. From the information garnered, team members can explore further possible patterns that may be emerging. At relevant times during the course of the meetings you conduct, you may find extensions of this analysis quite useful, depending on the task at hand. For example, making lists under pairs of columns headed "does" and "does not" or "will" and "will not" could be quite productive.

27. Using a Matrix Diagram

AN OLD BROOM SWEEPS CLEAN

In a Nutshell

A simple L-shaped matrix is used to explore new uses for an old object. Following this game, participants consider the problems they're trying to solve by using the matrix to elicit new possibilities.

Time

7 minutes.

What You'll Need

Flip chart and marking pens; participants will need paper and pens.

What to Do

1. Use as an example a simple broom. Down the left side of the "L," list the uses of the broom. Across the top, list the parts of it. The diagram will look as shown on the top of the next page.

2. Consider each part listed across the top in relation to each of the uses listed down the side. Use a symbol to indicate the strength of the existing or possible use as

Parts of Broom

Uses of Broom (vertical axis label)

strong, *some*, or *weak*. Typically, the following symbols are used:

- Strong relationship or use ◐
- Some relationship or use ☐
- Weak relationship or use ○

One new possible use that might emerge, for example, is that the top of the broom, when considered with the function of cleaning the floor, might lead to the development of a screw-on sponge attachment so that the same tool can be used as both a broom and a mop.

4. For the next five minutes, have participants consider a situation with which they are dealing in the meeting. Form an L-shaped matrix and establish the two sets of elements. Then, have participants use symbols to indicate possible patterns or new uses or priorities.

Background/Applications

The matrix is especially useful for comparing a number of elements. By arranging them into two sets, the elements in one can be aligned with each of the elements of the other and viewed in terms of viable combinations. Such diagrams are widely applicable to situations that participants will encounter at meetings.

Depending on the sets of information, you may wish to designate the traditional symbols in other ways: *negative impact, neutral impact, no impact* or *primary function, some use, new possibility.*

28. Finding Root Cause with the Five–Why Technique

THEORY Y AND "WHY"

Why?
Why?
Why?
Why?
Why?

In a Nutshell

You and a volunteer role-play a scenario in which a participant is upset over something. The five-why technique is used to uncover the root cause of his or her anger. Then each participant writes down something that might disturb him or her. The papers are collected and redistributed. Triads are then formed for further role-plays, with one person serving as the observer. The game illustrates the use of an excellent tool for probing until a root cause is determined. The tool, of course, can be used at numerous points during the meeting.

Time

5 minutes.

What You'll Need

Participants will need paper and pens. (Optional: two coupons for video rental, awarded to the Best Actors in a Role-Play.)

What to Do

1. Ask for a volunteer to do a little spontaneous play-acting with you. You begin along these lines. "Jim, I sense you're concerned about this." The volunteer replies, "You're darn right. The decision to _____ bothers me." (The volunteer can fill in the blank with anything.)

2. You'll continue from there, gently probing to learn the root cause of the person's concern, asking "Why?" five times until you get at what's really bothering the individual.

3. After the two-minute demonstration, ask participants to write down something regarding the meeting or the task that is bothering them or that might be a cause of concern in the future.

4. Collect the papers and spread them out face down on the table. Divide the participants into triads, with two role-players and one observer. Arrange the role-playing so that the least quiet person in the triad is the one who has to answer the "Why?" questions.

5. This person chooses a paper from the center of the table and uses what's written as the opening line. For example, "I'm concerned about the way votes are handled." The second role-player tries to get at root cause via "Why?" questions. The observer takes notes for later feedback. (Optional: Have the observers meet to decide who earned the acting "awards.")

Background/Applications

Students of business management are familiar with the name Douglas McGregor of M.I.T., who coined the terms Theory X and Theory Y in his much-acclaimed *The Human Side of Enterprise.* He posited that, according to Theory Y, the average person considers work a natural and normal part of life-not something to be avoided. Further, he said, the average person wants to do a good job and does not need threats to do so. He also felt the traditional work setting was not allowing for optimization of human potential.

Optimization occurs when people focus their energies on the core of a problem and not on interesting but irrelevant aspects of the problem. The five-why technique, attributed to Taiichi Ohno of the Toyota Motor Company, allows them to get at the real problem.

To avoid sounding repetitive or even pushy when using this monosyllabic question, put it in different syntactical structures. For example, instead of "Why?" ask, "What causes you to feel this way?" or something similar.

If you feel about your meeting participants as McGregor did about most employees, that they are committed to productive outcomes and that their potential is not fully realized, you can draw out the best from them by encouraging them to use the five-why method—first as a game to raise their comfort level and on later occasions as a tool that helps them get to the root of a problem.

29. *Working with a Fishbone Diagram*

THE CAUSE BONE'S CONNECTED TO THE EFFECT BONE

In a Nutshell

The fishbone diagram is an excellent way to explore the causes of a given effect. It helps participants consider the many possible reasons why something is occurring and then isolate the one cause they should focus on in order to improve the observed effect. Basically, participants isolate the effect and then list broad categories of factors that might be causing it.

Time

5-7 minutes.

What You'll Need

A bowl filled with fish-shaped cheese crackers; Post-it® notes measuring 2 x 1½ inches; flip chart and marking pens; a large drawing on the flip chart representing a fish skeleton, as shown on the next page.

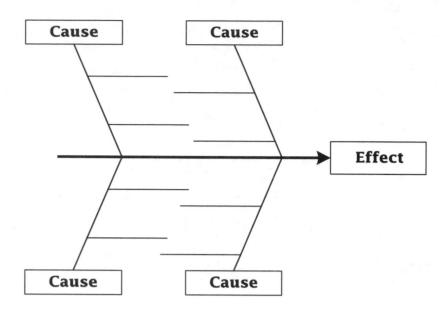

What to Do

1. Before the meeting, place the bowl of fish crackers in the center of the meeting table.

2. Write the ever-present problem of stress in the effect box (fish head). Give each participant two Post-it® notes and ask them to anonymously write two possible specific causes for stress in their workplace. One cause will be true; the other will be a phony.

3. As they're writing, label the four cause boxes with the following categories: Job Expectations, Environment, Coworkers, and Miscellaneous. Then have the participants affix their Post-it® notes on the appropriate lines (fishbones).

4. For fun, ask for a volunteer to determine which notes are true specific causes and which are phonies. Award him or her the bowl of crackers, no matter how many lies he or she was able to detect.

   (Note: You can extend the fun factor by capitalizing on your participants' assumptions. If they're like most meeting participants, they'll assume you've put the bowl of treats there as snacks. You can have fun with this assumption by pointing out that experts say most assumptions we make in relation to a problem are unfounded or erroneous. Here's how. Pretend to be busy for a moment or two before starting the meeting. As soon as anyone grabs a handful of crackers, feign horror and declare, "Oh, no! Those were supposed to be the prize for the truth-or-lie game!" Briefly caution against making assumptions when solving problems. Segue into the fishbone tool by saying it helps people reduce assumptions by examining effects and the factors that may be causing them.)

Background/Applications

The fishbone diagram is also known as the cause-and-effect diagram or the Ishikawa diagram, after its originator, Kaoru Ishikawa. Simple but effective, the diagram can be used for three different purposes:

1. The fishbone can be used when an effect has already been identified ("low morale," for example), for meeting participants to come up with possible broad causes for this effect. The effect is written on the head of the fish. Then, the broad cause categories are written at the out-side ends of the strong, diagonal bone lines attached to the spine. Next, specifics are written on the fine bone lines along each of the strong lines. So, if "Management" were listed as a broad cause category, some of the finer lines along that diagonal might contain these words: "withholds information," "makes excessive demands," "criticizes publicly." After all the specific examples are list-ed in each of the broad categories, the team would decide which one or two specifics they want to tackle.

2. The fishbone can also be used with a desired outcome. For example, if a group of workers wanted more recogni-tion for their efforts, they would list this outcome on the head of the fish. Then, they could label categories such

as "Make Presentations," "Communicate Upwards," "Win an Award," "Appear in a Publication," and so on. Participants would then suggest steps to be taken in each category and then vote on which plan to implement first.

3. The fishbone diagram can also be used to discern patterns, when it's not immediately obvious to meeting participants exactly what the problem is. If, for example, the participants are concerned about turnover rates, they might begin by listing 30 or 40 possible reasons. Once the list is complete, they would approach the diagram backwards: instead of identifying the cause categories and then listing the particulars, they would take their list of particulars and then determine the broad categories they form.

30. Employing the Force Field Analysis

LEWIN'S LIVING LINES

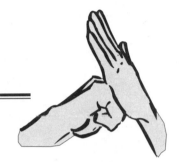

In a Nutshell

This game takes psychologist Kurt Lewin's simple lines, known as the force field analysis, and asks two teams to form living columns. These columns represent the driving forces and the restraining forces that form the famous line diagram, ideal for solving the problems that meeting participants are expected to solve.

Time

5-10 minutes.

What You'll Need

Four pages of flip chart paper (or computer-generated banners), with the following sentences or phrases: 1) "Current State: 2% of respondents in Pogo.com on-line survey are willing to occasionally forgo meals," 2) "Ideal State: Every person in this room would forgo a meal once a month and donate the money to charity," 3) "Driving Forces," and 4) "Restraining Forces." Also: masking tape, sheets of typing paper.

What to Do

1. Explain how the force field analysis works. Visually, it's a T-shaped construct. On the top is written the current state or situation. On the next line is the ideal state or situation. The left-hand column contains the driving forces—those elements that will help participants achieve the ideal state. The right-hand column contains the restraining forces—those elements that are causing the existing problem and preventing participants from reaching the ideal state.

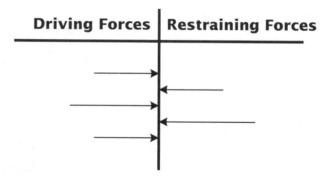

Driving Forces | **Restraining Forces**

2. On the wall, hang the banner with "Current State: 2% of respondents in Pogo.com on-line survey are willing to occasionally forgo meals." Beneath it hang the banner with "Ideal State: Every person in this room would forgo a meal once a month and donate the money to charity." Use masking tape to create a horizontal line beneath these two banners and then a vertical line to create the "T" structure of the force field analysis diagram.

3. Divide the class in two teams, the Drivers and the Restrainers. Allow five minutes for the Drivers to come up with things that will help a group reach the ideal and the Restrainers to think of reasons why the current state exists. They should write down one on each sheet of typing paper. Then, the members of each team take a sheet each and tape it to themselves. Once labeled, the Drivers stand on the left side of the T and the Restrainers stand

on the right. Members of one team cannot do a "reverse" of a label worn by a member of the other team; in other words, the labeled items must be original and not simply mirror images of what the other team has written.

4. Call time after five minutes. Whichever team has more living, labeled items in its column wins.

Background/Applications

Psychologist Kurt Lewin created this problem-solving tool, which is widely used because it's simple and it can help meeting participants zero in on the course of action most likely to produce the results they're seeking.

To achieve best outcomes, as the meeting leader, you'll have to invest some time before using this tool in a meeting. You'll have to research the current state of affairs. For example, there may currently be an error rate of 17% in the processing of requisitions. Ideally, the error rate could be reduced to 1%.

You'll want to speak with others before suggesting an ideal state. You want a goal that's attainable but challenging, realistic and yet ideal. Discuss the ideal state with others and then let your meeting participants decide what they feel they can achieve.

When recording the driving and restraining forces, it's important not to let the right column become a reflection of the left. For example, if you identify "more funding" as a driving force, you should not then identify a restraining force as "not enough funding."

Finally, once there are at least eight items in each column, the team should decide which one from either column represents the best use of their time and energy. They should then begin to identify the steps that can be taken to achieve the ideal state or remove the obstacles.

31. Making Storyboards

BORED? TRY BOARDING!

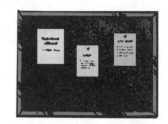

In a Nutshell

Storyboards offer problem-solvers a way to break down the problem and deal with it in segments. The meeting participants move from flip chart to flip chart, each of which contains one aspect of the problem.

Time

6 minutes.

What You'll Need

Flip chart and marking pens; masking tape; one package of Post-it® notes for each participant; participants will need pens.

What to Do

1. Identify a problem the group is dealing with. Write it on a sheet of chart paper and tape it to the wall.

2. Invite participants to break the problem down into at least three components. Write each component on a separate sheet of chart paper and tape the papers to the wall.

3. Divide the participants up into groups, placing one in front of each component. Hand each participant a package of Post-it® notes and a pen.

4. Ask them to come up with possible solutions (individually or as a group). They write these ideas on the Post-it® notes, one idea per note, and then stick them to the flip chart. After one minute, each group should move on to the next chart.

5. Spend the last two minutes synthesizing possible solutions or—if the group has produced a large quantity—have one participant synthesize the notes during the break. (If time permits, the synthesis could be presented at the next meeting.)

Background/Applications

The mind is not only an awful thing to waste; it's an awesome thing to replicate. Scientists estimate that a machine that matches our mental capacity would occupy most of the Empire State Building and cost $10 billion to produce. While its power seems infinite, the mind needs help from time to time. Storyboarding provides that help, providing a means for breaking down a large and complex issue.

It's a strategy at least as old as the ancient Romans, who recommended, "Divide et impera"—"Divide and conquer." When a team faces a large problem or task, it can often break it down and overcome the difficulties.

32. Eliciting Improvement Strategies

THE JAPANESE BATHTUB

In a Nutshell

The fun participants will have with this game is a derivative benefit; the primary purpose is to demonstrate that small groups can generate a large number of viable ideas in a small amount of time. Not only can this technique be used throughout the meeting, it can and should be used by managers to involve their employees.

Time

7 minutes.

What You'll Need

Flip chart and marking pens; participants will need paper and pens.

What to Do

1. Mention that many firms today use atypical interview techniques, including the group interview. For example, some interviewers take a group of applicants, assign them a collective task, and then sit in the back of the room to see how they solve it.

Explain that the game is similar to the interview technique but has a different purpose: you want to show that many workable ideas a group can generate in a very short time.

2. Give the group two minutes to figure out ways to improve a bathtub. (One person can serve as recorder.)

3. Call time after two minutes. Ask, "If our organization were in the business of producing bathtubs, do you think we could have gotten some ideas for improving our product from your two minutes of thinking?" The answer is invariably affirmative. (You may ask the recorder to read an example or two.)

4. For the final three minutes, present a problem the group is dealing with or will have to deal with. Write it on the flip chart and quickly elicit ideas for solving it.

Background/Applications

Many managers know there's great potential value in the ideas of those closest to the work—and great risks in not tapping into that source.

One of the best examples of this is the Frank Enos story, as reported by Geoffrey Brewer in *Performance*. The former CEO of Xerox, David Kearns, was addressing 3000 employees— "standard corporate stuff."

During the question-and-answer session, something startling happened: an hourly worker criticized the CEO! He accused him of not caring enough to talk to the production workers, who could have told him what the problems were with a certain product and why they were occurring.

There was a moment of total silence. Then, something just as startling: the CEO actually agreed with the criticism and promised things would change. And they did. Nine years later, when the President invited Kearns to Washington to accept the Malcolm Baldrige National Quality Award, guess who accompanied the CEO? That's right, Frank Enos!

If you're not soliciting ideas from each participant, if you're not encouraging managers to solicit ideas from each subordinate, you and the organization are missing out!

33. *Using a Multi-Pronged Approach*

HARD-TO-COUNT HANDSHAKES

In a Nutshell

Pose a problem to the group. In all likelihood, their answers will be numerous and quick ... and incorrect. Participants will probably give up after you tell them three or four times that they've not solved the problem. You'll then reveal the purpose of the game by explaining how three difficult approaches might have yielded the correct answer. Finally, you'll identify a problem they are facing and discuss possible approaches to its solution.

Time

7 minutes.

What You'll Need

Flip chart and marking pens; participants will need paper and pens. (Optional: token prize related to hands or handshakes, such as a nail clipper, an emery board, nail polish, or a tube of hand cream.)

What to Do

1. Present this problem. There are eight people gathering in

a room. Because they've not met each other, each person shakes hands with every other person, just once. What is the total number of handshakes?

2. Participants will shout out answers. Say, "Sorry, that's incorrect" each time until you hear the correct answer: 28. Ask the person giving the correct answer how he or she arrived at that figure. Award the prize and then proceed to explain that there are two other ways that any one of them could have come up with the answer. (Note: If nobody provides the correct answer within the first two minutes of the game, give the answer and then show the three possible ways to solve it.)

3. The hands-on, physically involved problem-solvers may have figured, "Well, there are eight of us in the meeting. Why don't we just start shaking each other's hands and count the number?" The more creative or visually oriented may have drawn eight stick figures and then sketched arrows to represent Figure 1 shaking with Figure 2, with Figure 3, and so on. Finally, the mathematically inclined may have solved the problem with this formula:

$$\frac{n\,(n\text{-}1)}{2}$$

4. For the remaining three minutes, identify a problem the group is dealing with and write it on the flip chart. Then elicit ideas for different ways to approach the problem.

Background/Applications

H.L. Mencken once noted, "For every complex problem there is an answer that is clear, simple, and wrong." Those tempted to jump in and solve problems without much forethought or afterthought are not likely to come up with the correct or the best solution.

To slow down the thinking process, it helps to have people of differing but equally appreciated skills. Psychologist J.P. Guilford, in his *Structure of the Intellect Model*, labeled 124 separate and discrete intelligences in his "cube of intellect." Unfortunately, we tend to prize the verbal and mathematical and ignore the rest.

Of course, you could poll your meeting participants to find out who can do what or you could leave it open to discussion which approach to use.

34. Viewing Problems as Opportunities

RESTATE THE STATE (OF THE PROBLEM)

In a Nutshell

Sooner or later, every meeting participant gets discouraged. If discouragement is widespread, however, or if the discouragement appears early in the meeting process, you may find it difficult to keep your group united. With difficult problems or assignments, it helps to find the hidden opportunities embedded in the situation. That's what participants will do with this game.

Time

6 minutes.

What You'll Need

Flip chart and marking pens.

What to Do

1. Acknowledge that some members may already be feeling discouraged by the enormity of the assignment given to the group.

2. Remind them of sayings like "Every cloud has a silver lining" and "It's always darkest before the dawn." Share with them a time in your own life when something you initially thought was a cross to bear turned out to be a blessing in disguise. Ask if someone would like to share a similar experience.

3. Then proceed to give one example of how the problem they're facing may turn out to have unforeseen benefits for them as individuals and as a group—benefits apart from the outcome. For example, if the assigned task is something about which they don't know much (yet)—such as benchmarking or setting up a focus group—they'll learn a lot in the process. That's a distinct benefit.

4. Write the benefit on the flip chart and elicit two more. Keep these posted throughout the meeting as the group explores the problem.

Background/Applications

In the words of General Colin Powell, "Perpetual optimism is a force multiplier." In addition to the many other duties you face as meeting leader, it's important to maintain the "esprit du corps." This game will elicit some positive elements with which you can motivate the group. There are other things you can do:

■ Meet with naysayers one on one and explain how corrosive a negative attitude can be.

■ Arrange for a high-level executive to stop by and express appreciation for the work the group is doing and/or will do.

■ Occasionally, express your own admiration, but be careful not to overdo it. Effusive praise not only embarrasses people, but also tends to make them suspect the sincerity of the person bestowing the praise.

■ "Police" expressions of discouragement or disparagement

by issuing a whistle to each participant and encouraging them to blow it on anyone who's being unduly critical.

Remind the group that the toughest things we do are often the most important or most valuable. Cite the Peace Corps slogan ("the toughest job you'll ever love"), the fight-back spirit following the attack on the World Trade Center ("You can break our hearts but never our spirit!"), and the research done by Mihaly Csikszentmihalyi, who found that optimal experiences almost always centered on meeting a difficult challenge.

35. Appreciating Differences in Thinking Style

CONVERGE OR DIVERGE?

In a Nutshell

The purpose of this game is learning about thinking styles. Participants are asked several questions, the answers to which will indicate their style. You wrap up by asserting the benefit of such mental diversity.

Time

7 minutes.

What You'll Need

Participants will need paper and pens. (Optional: for the divergent thinkers, an atypically shaped object, such as a box of straws with a curl in them or a pencil that is curved.)

What to Do

1. Tell the group you'd like to ask them a series of quick questions. Ask that they record their answers and that they bear with you as they do so.

2. Begin with "From everything you've heard or read or been taught, how do you get to heaven?"

3. Pause a few seconds and then ask, "How can you tell someone is getting old?"

4. When they're ready, ask, "Assume you've taken your family on vacation to a national park. And now ... your six-year-old son is missing. You rush up to the forest ranger, who assures you with these words: 'Every day, we average seven lost kids. But in the 43 years since the park's been open, we've found every one of them! So I know we'll find your child. But there's a problem. Typically, we have seven, but today we're missing 15 kids. So I cannot commit all my resources to your child alone. Please choose: would you like us to send the helicopter over the area where the child was last seen or would you like me to send the foot patrol into that area?'"

4. Ask: "For question #1, did anyone have an answer other than 'You need to follow the Golden Rule' or something similar?" If anyone did, call on that person. Use his or her answer as an example of the difference between convergent thinking (typical, logical, empirical, predictable, experiential) and divergent thinking (unexpected, creative, unusual, often humorous, sometimes absurd, innovative). Award a token prize at this time if you wish. If no one had an example of divergent thinking, share something a child might have said: "You need a really huge trampoline" or "You go to hell and take a left."

5. Do the same with the second question. You'll hear the typical answers: gray hair, knees give out, eyesight weakens. Ask for a divergent answer and reward it with a token prize. Share some examples of divergent thinking, some things children might have observed, such as "They start to get ugly" or "Their mouths move before the words come out."

6. Finally, explain that those who chose the foot patrol are probably detail-oriented types, who are logical, analytical, precise. They are disciplined and see their tasks through

to completion. They tend to think convergently. The helicopter people, by contrast, are more likely to see the big picture and thus are more tempted to go off in a number of directions. They're not especially good at following through but they're great at coming up with new ideas. They're creative and spontaneous and visionary.

7. You can do a quick assessment by asking, "Did anyone have all three convergent answer or all three divergent?" No matter what the results, explain that it's better to have a mix rather than a group made up of people who all think the same way.

Background/Applications

According to Alfred W. Munzert, author of *Test Your IQ*, "Highly creative and highly intelligent individuals function with good balance in development and interaction between the two halves of the brain." It's true that many of us depend on one thinking style or the other—convergent or divergent—but there are some who are able to draw upon both convergent and divergent skills. Sometimes, they can do this drawing simultaneously, capitalizing on an interdependency of functions. Those who can are known as *lateralized* thinkers. A quick and easy way to illustrate how readily we use one thinking style or the other is to show the following diagram and ask, "What letter clearly, visibly, obviously does not fit with the others?"

$$c \qquad d$$
$$t$$
$$e \qquad j$$

Convergent, logical, analytical thinkers will quickly say "j," with their rationale being that the letter is out of sequence. The big-picture, divergent thinkers will say "t," the letter not found in one of the four quadrants. (If possible, draw the t-shape using a different color of magic marker, to make the distinction even more clear.)

36. Exploring Problems from a Different Viewpoint

MOTHER NATURE SAVES FATHER TIME

In a Nutshell

In this game, participants will have a chance to select a role and think as someone in that role might think. In this way they can develop other-person thinking, which is one purpose of this game. The process can also lead the meeting members to some concrete leads as they work to solve their common problem.

Time

5 minutes.

What You'll Need

Flip chart and marking pens; participants will need paper and pens.

What to Do

1. Begin with a reference to the time in American history when polio was a national nightmare. (Some participants may actually remember some details of that time.) Share the fact that when Jonas Salk, who discovered the polio

vaccine, was asked by a reporter how he had succeeded, he replied, "I learned to think the way Mother Nature thinks."

2. Have these words (and others you may wish to include) written in advance about eight inches from the top of the flip chart: Police Officer - Athlete - Our Senior Management - Nun - Gardener - Nurse - Social Worker - Pilot - City Planner - Golfer - Therapist - Librarian - Marine Biologist - Cardiologist - Journalist - Janitor - Skier - Secretary - Politician - Child. Then write the problem the group is currently working on.

3. Have participants work in pairs or triads for four minutes. They are to select one of the roles or positions listed on the flip chart and examine the problem as this sort of person might.

4. For the last minute or so, ask for workable ideas that emerged from the game.

Background/Applications

Aristotle noted, more than two millennia ago, "Man is the most imitative of living creatures, and through imitation learns his earliest lessons." All too often, unfortunately, we stay within our comfort zones and thus fail to experience the headiness that comes from new experiences.

For the meeting leader, this headiness can be spawned by encouraging participants to get inside the heads of people unlike themselves, unlike those with whom they typically associate.

Once there, they can learn some lessons by imitating the thinking styles of those individuals, attending to the various aspects of the situation that would concern different people. (A situation viewed from the eyes of a police officer, for example, might have security elements that the artist, concerned with visual harmony, might not even notice.)

37. Testing Assumptions

THE DAILY DOUBLE

In a Nutshell

It's been said that about 50% of the assumptions we hold are erroneous. This quick game serves as a prelude to stripping assumptions away from an actual problem on which the group is working. It asks particpants to make some assumptions in answer to questions you pose. Afterwards, when the group learns how invalid their assumptions are, you'll probe a meeting-related issue by exploring the assumptions surrounding it.

Time

6 minutes.

What You'll Need

Flip chart and marking pens; participants will need paper and pens.

What to Do

1. Ask participants to jot down their answers to these three questions:
   a) If I were to give you a penny today, two pennies tomor-

row, four pennies the next day, and eight pennies the next day—in other words, if I were to start with a penny and double the amount every day for 30 days— would you assume your total at the end of the month would be above a thousand dollars, above one hundred thousand, or above a million?

b) What do you assume the word "quidnunc" means: a miser, a gossip, a member of the clergy, or a scientist?

c) In regard to workplace violence, what would you assume is the number of Americans killed each week on the job: 2 every day, 20 every week, 200 every month, or 2000 every year?

2. Go over the answers: a) above a million, b) a gossip, c) 20 every week. Point out how dangerous it is to make assumptions and then believe we know what we're talking about.

3. On the flip chart, write the issue or problem the group is assembled to deal with. Then, for the remaining three minutes, elicit some assumptions participants are holding regarding this issue. Challenge those assumptions when you can or verify them or suggest further investigation to test the validity of the assumptions.

Background/Applications

This simple exercise, ideally, gets participants thinking about relying on assumptions, many of which will be erroneous. If you're able to challenge the assumptions surrounding the meeting issue, you'll succeed in bringing the group a step closer to attaining your goal.

The transcendental chiding from Ralph Waldo Emerson ("A foolish consistency is the hobgoblin of little minds") remains good advice to this day. Some of our beliefs should be periodically challenged and, when appropriate, relinquished.

To be sure, there are some central beliefs we will never give up. Losing faith, for example, in one's family, one's government, one's company, is fundamentally disturbing. But losing faith in beliefs that limit us is a kind of mental housekeeping that can have multiple benefits.

38. Analyzing Data with a Correlation Chart

KEEPING THE MEETING WORLD ON ITS AXIS

In a Nutshell

Because data-collection is a lengthy process, this game operates with data already collected. Its purpose is to show how the correlation works: it shows the relationship between two variables. Award applause, if not a token prize, to the small group that first makes sense of the data provided by charting it. Use the game as a transition to the data to be analyzed regarding the situation the participants need to study.

Time

7 minutes.

What You'll Need

Handout #1; participants will need paper and pens.
(Optional: token prizes of graph paper for the winners.)

What to Do

1. Explain what a correlation chart is and how it works. Say

that later in the meeting (or in future meetings) the group will have a chance to examine data and analyze the possible relationships among them. Tell participants you have a game to show them how to construct the graph and interpret the data.

2. Distribute the handout (pages 116-117) and encourage small groups to work together for four minutes. The final chart will look like this:

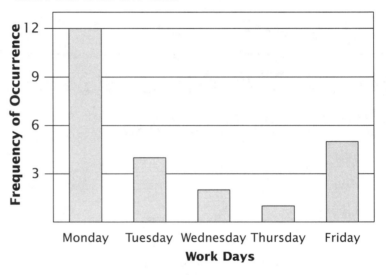

3. Once a winner has been declared, point out that Mondays in and of themselves, of course, don't cause workplace accidents. However, there may be some things associated with Monday that are leading to a higher number of accidents than on any other day. It might be, for example, that coworkers who haven't seen each other for a few days are so busy catching up on each other's weekends that they're not paying as much attention as they should to the work at hand. Elicit other possibilities.

4. Launch into the type of data you would like the members to consider (or gather, if they'll be meeting again). Make certain to note that the charted results will give them things to consider. The chart will have not answers, but simply more questions to be raised and examined before the group can solve the problem or improve the situation.

Background/Applications

The use of data minimizes reliance on opinion, which can be a source of conflict. Further, the opinion of an especially vocal or otherwise influential individual can distort reality. If such a person claims the organization has a morale problem, for example, it may be just that this one person is having a morale problem—but, if he or she is persuasive, the group may be convinced this is the problem they need to attend to before going on to improve processes. However, if a survey of employees were conducted, it might reveal most don't consider poor morale a problem. The facts, as they say, speak for themselves.

You'll have to gather data well in advance of the meeting (or ask selected participants to do so) to ensure the meeting participants can start analyzing the situation. Allow discussion, yes, but don't allow veteran employees to sway others when they say their experience is more reliable than the data. Collecting and analyzing data will help the group define the problem it needs to be pursuing and, thus, save everyone's time. Both quantitative and qualitative information have a bearing on any given problem. The quantitative data are measurements; they are metrics, as opposed to anecdotal reports or opinion.

The correlation chart involves numbers. The numerical relationship does not prove that one event causes another (a causal relationship); it suggests areas for further scrutiny. You'll use it when you need to find links between two variables that you suspect may have a bearing on one another.

Accident Log

Directions: You're part of a group assembled to improve the situation of workplace accidents. You've been given the following alphabetical report detailing the accidents that occurred in the last week (October 3-7). Your job is to prepare a correlation chart that has two axes. The horizontal (X) axis will show the time frame and the vertical (Y) axis will show the number of accidents. You will have four minutes to prepare the chart.

- Julio Accedo dropped a typewriter he was moving and injured his foot on Oct. 3.

- Gwen Broxton caught her finger in the printed while replacing a cartridge on Oct. 7.

- Terry Buscemi fell off his chair at a meeting on Oct. 3, spraining his ankle.

- Gail Carruthers spilled acetone on Oct. 5 and inhaled toxic fumes.

- Erika Danziger fractured a bone in her arm when all the drawers of a file cabinet opened when it tipped over on Oct. 4.

- Jim Dollinger fell down the stairs during the fire drill on Oct. 3.

- Elvira Dutton cut herself while using a letter-opener on Oct. 7.

- Gerry Ellis inadvertently punctured himself with a pencil point on Oct. 6.

- Juan Fulton, while washing a counter top in the break room, got a sliver in his finger on Oct. 3.

- Tennika Garrison spilled hot coffee in her lap on Oct. 4.

- Robert Halston fell off a ladder while changing a bulb on Oct. 3.

- Victor Iannacone tripped on the entryway rug on Oct. 7.

- Frank Jackson's left foot was run over in the warehouse on Oct. 3.

- Serita Kelly suffered a sprain when her foot was caught in a hole on the front lawn on Oct. 7.

- Linda Koonz reported bathroom disinfectant spray irritated her eyes on Oct. 3.

- Sheldon Levine tripped on a rug in the conference room on Oct. 7.

Accident Log (continued)

- Gabriella Milstein jumped up when she heard a loud noise and struck her head on the wall file on Oct. 4.

- Ahren Mulroney reported a back strain when he lifted boxes off the delivery truck on Oct. 3.

- Miguel Nobrega stapled his finger on Oct. 3 and drew blood.

- Sally Ollenstein was injured when cartons from the top shelf fell on her on Oct. 3.

- Paul Roberson was involved in a forklift accident on Oct. 5.

- Sara Ruggles slid on the rug protector and fell on Oct. 3.

- Elizabeth Shin suffered a paper cut on Oct. 4.

- Anthony Yashida burned himself on the break room stove on Oct. 3.

Part Five

MAKING SURE EVERYONE'S OPINION IS HEARD

It's been observed that good listening is what separates the mediocre company from the excellent company. If managers are serious about excellence, if they truly seek to convert innovative thought into organizational realities, if they are determined to optimize employee potential and make workers feel valued, then they must find a means of both soliciting employee input and responding to it. The same is true in the microcosm of the meeting.

When contributions are devalued or derided, when quieter members are ignored, when the most verbal members are the most recognized, the meeting process is undermined. And the results of poor listening can be powerful in their negative impact. With the games in this section, you will find numerous ways of harnessing listening power for positive impact.

The very first game ensures everyone is heard from: you are "penalized" if you don't call on each person present within the first five minutes. With the second game, opinions and ideas are solicited via input to an affinity diagram. With the third, opinions are elicited via a survey.

The fourth game, "Taking an Idea Through Three Stages," ensures that an idea travels through three stages, so that no member can kill an idea in its infancy, before it's had a chance to develop. In the next game, a concept that has been developed is reduced to its basic essence, as a way of ensuring that the primary focus is not distorted, diminished, or filtered. The sixth game uses a "Simon says" type of misdirection to test listening skills. The final game uses a simple but effective technique to get opinions from every member of the group.

39. Calling on Everyone by Name

THE INCLUSION CONCLUSION

In a Nutshell

This game not only ensures that everyone's opinion is heard, but also helps personalize interactions, because you address participants by name. A volunteer observes you to ensure that you do so.

Time

5 minutes.

What You'll Need

3 x 5 cards (one for each participant) and marking pens; a timer. (Optional: token prizes or refreshments in case you lose your bet.)

What to Do

1. Have every participant write his or her name on a card, even if you already know their names. Give the cards to a volunteer sitting at the opposite end of the table, who will spread the names in front of him or her. Set the timer for five minutes.

2. Explain that as a meeting leader you try to hear from

every participant—and you try to address them by name. Declare that you bet you can do that in the first five minutes.

3. Continue with the meeting. As it progresses, you make a deliberate effort to ask to hear from each participant, calling on each by name. As you do so, the volunteer quietly removes the card of that person.

4. By the time the timer goes off, there should be no cards left. If there are any, you lose: distribute the token prizes.

Background/Applications

Names are important to us. Most people are offended if you fail to remember their names or you call them by the wrong name. As meeting leader, you should be able to quickly enough commit the names of your participants to memory. Beyond that, though, you need to call upon everyone by name—equally—throughout the course of the meeting.

If meetings are to succeed, you must nurture the fragile ecosystem of each meeting. This means being vigilant about ideas being proposed: those that receive no response, like all new growths, will wither and die on the meeting vine and those who propose them may easily vow not to bother sharing other thoughts later.

Not only do you have to listen, but you also have to ensure others are listening as well. Consider inviting an outsider to the meeting, as an observer, to assess the listening skills of participants.

Here are some possibilities for improving your own listening skills:

- Compare yourself with the best listener you've ever known. Analyze what makes him or her so effective and then try to incorporate elements of that style into your own.

- For one full week, ask others—peers, supervisors, customers, suppliers, even meeting participants—to assess your listening skills. (It'll help if you prepare a simple form for them to use.) Four weeks later, ask the same people if they've noticed any improvement in your style.

- Periodically restate what you think you've heard. If you've not fully understood the other person's concept, ask them to explain it.

- Force yourself to listen without interruption.

- Ask questions—both simple and complex.

- Avoid judging the speaker on the basis of appearance, age, position, gender, and any prior knowledge you have of him or her.

- Actively work to increase your attention span.

40. Using an Affinity Diagram

HAVE A MINI-AFFINI TEA

In a Nutshell

This short interaction yields valuable information for determining the flow of events relative to the meeting purpose. Participants engage in a "brain dump," using 3 x 5 cards or Post-it® notes. They then organize the cards or notes into categories.

Time

5 minutes

What You'll Need

3 x 5 cards or Post-it® notes (five for each participant); flip chart and marking pens; participants will need paper and pens. (Optional: herbal tea and paper cups.)

What to Do

Optional: To add an element of fun, serve tea to those who wish it and explain that the group has been assembled for an "Affini Tea," at which they'll explore a particular topic.

1. Review the purpose of the meeting, to ensure that all participants understand fully, and then explain that the

group needs to determine the steps that it will have to complete before it can meet the meeting goal.

2. Then allow two minutes for a "brain dump," during which each participant is to write down steps, one per card or note.

3. Collect the cards or notes and read them off, discarding duplicates and possibly combining those that are similar.

4. Spread the reduced number of cards or notes on the meeting table and have the group divide them into logical piles of activities.

5. Once they've done this, they should create a heading for each group. Discussion will occur throughout, so that, in time, the piles and the items within each will have a logical flow.

Background/Applications

Although Michael Brassard, author of *The Memory Jogger Plus+*, maintains that affinity diagrams elicit more "gut level" reactions than intellectual or logical responses, meeting leaders can use the process to elicit both types of responses. That process is efficient and democratic, for it requires all members to contribute.

Like many tools associated with the quality movement, this one originated in Japan in the 1960s. Then, a cultural anthropologist named Jiro Kawakita found himself drowning in a sea of details he had collected in his observation of different societies.

The affinity diagram serves several purposes; it is best used when you and the other meeting participants are grappling with large amounts of information. (Of course, as shown here, the information can be divided into smaller chunks and the affinity process can then be applied to the parts of the whole.) The process usually generates new slants, fresh perspectives, and unique solutions.

41. Surveying Opinions

SURVEINS

SURVEY CREW

In a Nutshell

You, as the meeting leader, prepare a questionnaire in advance, related to a specific problem on which the team has been stuck. Group members, in pairs, answer the questions and tabulate the results. A discussion is held, on the basis of which a second questionnaire is prepared.

Time

15-20 minutes.

What You'll Need

Handout #1; flip chart and marking pens; participants will need paper and pens. (Optional: token prizes, such as marking pens.)

What to Do

1. Distribute the handout (page 128). Give participants about five minutes to answer the questions related to a workplace issue. Then ask for a volunteer to be the recorder. (Option: Award him or her the token prize for volunteering.)

2. Next, begin a discussion of their survey answers; the recorder should write the most relevant points on the flip chart. Look for the main "veins" leading to the "heart" of the problem.

3. On the basis of those "veins," have the group develop a second survey. If time permits, ask the participants to form new pairs and answer the survey questions. (Note: The second questionnaire can be used at the next meeting. It can also be distributed to coworkers and managers who will not attend that next meeting.)

Background/Applications

The quality movement helped us see "customers" in a whole new light. The concepts of internal customer and external customer gave rise to the understanding that whoever receives the output of our work can rightfully be termed our "customer."

In a sense, your meeting participants are your customers. Accordingly, it's important to learn all you can about what they want, need, and expect so you can best give them what they're seeking. The questionnaire provides an excellent tool for such learning. In many ways, it's similar to the focus group that corporations employ to learn more about customer reactions to products and services.

John E. Jones, William L. Bearley, and Douglas C. Watsabaugh, authors of *The New Fieldbook for Trainers*, address the value of using focus groups to identify organizational needs and the value of using surveys for what they call "organizational sensing." They further recommend using a team setting. The "Surveins" game enables you to maximize the benefit of such meetings while minimizing the time typically required.

Surveins

Directions: Assume your group has been stuck on the issue of whether or not to hold a project management conference. At this meeting, your meeting leader has distributed the following questionnaire. Answer the questions as fully and honestly as possible. The members of your group will then share their answers and, from them, develop a second questionnaire.

1. What would be your primary objection to holding this conference?

2. Which of these issues do you think your coworkers need the most help with?
   - fundamentals of project management
   - monitoring of projects
   - troubleshooting
   - managing multiple projects
   - software
   - developing an action plan

3. How would you (and the other members of this committee) be involved if the conference were held?

4. How much and what kind of support would you need if you agreed to participate in planning such a conference?

5. What benefits do you feel could be derived from such a conference?

42. Taking an Idea Through Three Stages

PIPE-UP DREAMS

In a Nutshell

Participants are invited to speak up regarding their quietly held dreams. The group selects one dream and views it from a practical perspective. In the third stage, critics get to work evaluating, comparing, identifying omissions, planning next steps, etc. Sometimes such collaboration leads meeting participants back to the "dreamy" first stage. This process is used often in brainstorming sessions at places like Disneyland.

Time

5-10 minutes.

What You'll Need

Flip chart and marking pens; participants will need paper and pens. (Optional: three paper hats for each participant, labeled "Dreamer," "Pragmatist," and "Evaluator.")

What to Do

1. Ask participants to think of a dream they have in relation

to the workplace in general or in relation to the specific problem they've convened to assess. Their "dream" should represent an ideal state in which a particular problem has been solved with win/win benefits for all concerned. (You can use the example of the healthcare worker who dreamed that poor people would always be able to have the expensive medication they need. Her dream led her to organize a system whereby insurance-covered patients who had to stop taking their medications for some reason donated their pills to the needy.)

2. Record the dreams on a flip chart. Select one and ask the group to discuss it realistically, pragmatically.

3. Once a plan begins to emerge, switch gears: ask them to evaluate the dream, to identify roadblocks that must be overcome before the dream can be turned into reality. (Optional: To add an element of fun and to distinguish the move from one stage to another, have participants put on new hats each time.)

Background/Applications

Einstein once admitted, "When I examined myself and my methods of thought, I came to the conclusion that the gift of fantasy has meant more to me than my talent for absorbing knowledge." All too often in meetings, leaders tend to discard the wild ideas and members tend to scoff at them. This "Pipe-up Dreams" game ensures that neither reaction will occur.

But beyond fostering innovative thought and welcoming organization "lunatics," as Peter Drucker refers to them, there must be a taming of the wildness, the absurdity, the lunacy. Creativity consultant and author Geoffrey Hill posits that creativity and corporations create an "antithetical situation." And here's where the meeting leader comes in: "But with the proper leadership," he maintains, "we can institutionalize creative anarchy .... The right leader will help employees embrace anarchistic thinking."

43. Reducing a Concept to Its Essence

VERBUM SAT

In a Nutshell

This game helps develop the kind of bare-bones thinking prized by organizations. You'll need at least five other team members to play this game, one to be a timekeeper and the others to form two teams, then four teams. The pairs of teams (or individuals, if you have only five people at the meeting) will quiz each other, competing for points. (Optional: token prizes such as books or dictionaries make ideal prizes for those who demonstrate that "Verbum sat sapienti"—"A word to the wise is sufficient").

Time

5-7 minutes.

What You'll Need

Flip chart and marking pens; participants will need paper and pens.

What to Do

1. Begin by quoting the Latin phrase, "Verbum sat sapienti."

From there, point out the importance of identifying key components of an issue, so that time is focused on what matters most.

2. Explain that this game will have two teams (or individuals) on one side competing with two teams (or individuals) on the other side. Divide the group into two A teams and two B teams. Give each of the four teams four sheets of paper for carrying out these instructions: "Each team is to create four sets of identifiers and identities. These identities could be people connected to our meeting purpose or they could be things related in one way or another to our meeting purpose. Then you'll decide on four identifying phrases for each of the identities. In other words, you'll reduce each identity to its lowest common denominator, its basic essence. For example, if the identity is 'Marilyn Monroe,' the identifiers might be 'Happy Birthday,' 'Joe DiMaggio,' 'Norma Jean,' and 'Gentlemen Prefer Blondes.' Work quietly so the other teams can't hear your identities and identifiers."

3. Once they've finished, collect the 16 sheets. Give four from the A Team to the B1 Team. Take four from the B team and give them to the A1 Team.

4. Team A1 will read the identifiers from each sheet, one at a time, to Team A2, which will try to guess the identity. Team B1 will do the same with Team B2. The teams will have one and a half minutes. You and the timekeeper will keep track of the time, one for each pair of teams.

5. Then the teams reverse the process. Give Teams A2 and B2 the remaining sheets from the opposite teams, to use with Teams A1 and B1. Again, the teams have one and a half minutes.

6. Award the prizes to the A teams or the B teams that had more correct answers.

Background/Applications

On his deathbed, Minnesota Senator Hubert Humphrey spoke of his "irreducible essence." In other words, when all else is stripped away, what is it that defines a particular person? What is his or her elemental reason for being? For what does he or she wish to be remembered? Most of us would say something about our loved ones, as did Lee Iacocca when he answered this question. For Humphrey, though, it was love of country.

This ability to home in on an often-shifting target is critical for you as the meeting leader. You need to keep your members focused on a singular goal, despite the distractions, the conflicts, the inclinations to engage in "war stories" or to wander around the topic.

The efficiency of such strategizing was evident in the 1992 presidential campaign, when advisor James Carville coined the phrase, "It's the economy, stupid." Find an equally powerful (but less insulting) phrase that within seconds can focus your group's attention and energy on the task at hand. (The "Verbum Sat" game may have given you a few ideas.)

44. Developing Listening Skills

LISTEN UP!

In a Nutshell

You ask meeting participants a series of questions, then engage them in a simple activity that illustrates the point that many of us don't really hear what's said.

Time

5 minutes.

What You'll Need

No materials are required for this game.

What to Do

1. To illustrate the fact that we think we listen better than we do, call on one person and ask him or her the following questions. "Do you think of yourself as a good listener?" (The answer will almost always be in the affirmative.) "On a scale of 1-10, with 10 being high, how would you score yourself?" (The answer will usually be 6 or higher.) Then say, "Hmmm. Well, on a scale of 1-10, how would your wife/husband score you?"

2. Briefly discuss the importance of listening well in meet-

ings and then ask for a show of hands in response to each of the following five questions:

- "How many of you studied science in high school?"
- "How many of you studied history?"
- "How many of you studied a foreign language?"
- "How many studied math?"
- "How many studied listening?" (Very few, if any hands will go up, perhaps explaining why so many people admit to needing to improve their listening skills.)

3. Next, ask the participants to join you in a simple experiment. Raise your right hand in the air with the index finger extended and the others curled into a first and say, "Please do exactly as I tell you to do. Raise your hand now with one finger—preferably the index finger—pointing upward. Now form a circle—as I am doing—with the index finger and your thumb." (Pause a moment to be certain everyone is following.) "Next, just as I am doing, bring that circle closer and closer to your cheek until it's about one inch from your face." (Pause.) "Now I want everyone to do what I tell you: go right ahead and place that circle on your chin." Then place your fingers on your cheek. About half of the participants will do the same, even though you clearly said "chin" in your instructions.

Background/Applications

The tragic results that can result from poor listening are perhaps best illustrated by the story of Roger Boisjoly, a junior engineer who tried to warn others that a shuttle launch should not take place. He gave up, he later reported, "when it was apparent that I couldn't get anybody to listen." The outcome was the Challenger explosion.

You may wish to explore these questions with your meeting participants from time to time as a means of making them more aware of the need for good listening skills.

1. Do you watch facial expressions of others as you talk with them?

2. Does your expression show sincere interest?

3. Do you maintain eye contact throughout exchanges?

4. Do you give feedback to show you're interested? (How?)

5. Do you deliberately avoid interrupting others as they speak?

6. Do you maintain a comfortable distance from others?

7. Do you paraphrase to check your understanding?

8. Do you inquire about the feeling behind the words?

9. Do you work at not finishing sentences for other people?

10. Do you show respect for the opinions of others who disagree with your viewpoint?

45. Using the Crawford Technique

THE EASE OF C's

In a Nutshell

Ensuring input from every meeting participant is the primary purpose of the Crawford technique. You simply pose a question, address an issue, or define a problem—anything for which you'd like feedback. The participants respond in writing.

Time

7 minutes.

What You'll Need

Flip chart and marking pens; participants will need paper and pens.

What to Do

1. Write on the flip chart the topic under consideration.

2. Ask each participant to write down his or her thoughts about the topic or information that is pertinent and needs to be considered. (They can do so anonymously, if they wish.)

3. Collect the papers. Address the points one at a time, for the next several minutes.

Background/Applications

This remarkably simple, remarkably effective technique was named after C.C. Crawford of the University of Southern California—although people were no doubt using it long before his name was associated with it. The technique not only guarantees everyone a chance to voice his or her opinion, but also collects information that might not otherwise have been shared. In addition, the technique provides a starting point for discerning patterns or trouble spots that may be emerging.

Part Six

REACHING CONSENSUS

Many factors contribute to consensus. Among them, to be sure, are the meeting leader's personality and—to a lesser or greater extent—the personalities of the participants. The time factor has to be considered, as does the significance or merit of the proposal under consideration. Too much information or, conversely, too little information regarding the proposal can also impede the drive toward agreement. A number of techniques will help you help participants find an acceptable position that elicits positive responses on both the rational level (affirmed through analysis) and the intuitive level (endorsed through emotions, the feeling that the course of action is the right one to pursue).

The first game, "Achieving Compromise Positions," invites anonymous responses: participants declare that either they can live with the solution being proposed or they could live with it conditionally (i.e., after certain alterations are made). The second effects compromise through mediation: participants commit to abide by an outside mediator's decision regarding the proposal on which participants can't agree. The third game uses a storm analogy to preventing anger from disrupting the discussion, to help participants move past a conflict point and toward a compromise opinion.

The fourth game allows you to streamline the process of reaching consensus with your group through a vote on the nature of the stalemate. (Is it *content* or is it *context*?) The fifth game, "Assessing Futility," poses the question (with no cruelty intended), "Are we beating a dead horse?" It reminds them that repetition may work for memorization but it wastes time for meetings.

A novel twist on the consensus-reaching process can be found in the sixth game, "Employing Persuasion." A panel representing the "pro" position and then a panel representing the "con" attempt to persuade a judge. The group, ideally, will accept the judge's ruling, based on the merits of their efforts. The next game helps participants discover the depth of underlying feelings on a given issue; they write their feelings on cards, which are then collected and assessed by a volunteer. Often, the volunteer's report is a sufficient stimulus to shift positions so the group can finally achieve consensus. In the eighth game, "Allocating Assets," participants are given a dollar's worth of coins, which they then use to express the value they attach to subcomponents of the issue under consideration.

The last two games help participants to move beyond the cycle of votes that is all too often the only method used to achieve consensus. The A-D-D technique helps voters decide where the critical stumbling block lies: are there too few advantages to the proposal, too many disadvantages, or too many areas yet unexplored? The final game deals with a very serious issue: how deeply do participants feel about their position? They are asked to decide if they feel so strongly that they would rather disassociate from the group than proceed with a given course of action. If any one member votes to withdraw, the group then votes on what is more important: the integrity of the group or the push to move in a certain direction.

46. *Achieving Compromise Positions*

I COULD LIVE WITH IT IF ...

In a Nutshell

The purpose of this game is to effect compromise by asking participants to write down their position on a compromise under consideration: they can either "live with it" or agree to it if a specific change is made. The "position papers" are then counted and decisions are made, based upon the results. The written process offers some anonymity—perhaps only temporarily—and gives you a chance to learn the extent of support for the compromise position.

Time

5 minutes.

What You'll Need

Participants will each need a pen and two sheets of paper.

What to Do

1. Explain that the catch phrase used in consensus situations is "I can live with it." Typically, if all the meeting participants feel this way or better about a proposal, the group will usually go ahead and adopt it. Then explain

that you'd like to go beyond that position, if possible, by giving the group two choices.

2. Briefly propose a solution to a stalemate or restate a decision that seems to be a compromise.

3. Ask each person to write either "I can live with it" or "I could live with it if ...," completing the sentence by specifying the objection.

4. Collect and read the sheets. If an "I could live with it if ..." statement suggests a change that can easily be incorporated, say so. If the statement changes the compromise proposal substantially, lay it on the table for the group to reconsider. If the holdout cannot be swayed, you can either resort to majority rule at this point or try another consensus technique.

Background/Applications

Laboratory rats move quickly through mazes because they're motivated to get to the food they know awaits them at the end. In other circumstances, they've proven they can quickly learn to swim when it's question of survival. While the issue on which your meeting participants are stalled is likely not a matter of life or death, you stand a better chance of effecting compromise or reaching consensus when you can make the proposal worth their while. Allowing the "I can live with it if ..." input says to participants, in effect, "We don't want you to simply live with this proposal. We want you to live with it *willingly*." Holdouts are more likely to be willing to support a compromise or consensus when they are given the opportunity to provide further input and help refine the proposal, rather than being made to feel that the proposal is an all-or-nothing-at-all proposition.

47. *Using Mediation*

WHAT YOU HEAR IS WHAT YOU GET

In a Nutshell

Mediation is used when the participants cannot reach consensus. If they agree, the situation is taken to a neutral third party, whose judgment participants agree in advance to accept. You should approach this person before the meeting, to ask if you can call on him or her to serve in this role if necessary.

Time

7 minutes.

What You'll Need

An outsider who has considerable experience with the organization and who's well respected for being intelligent and fair; a speaker phone in the meeting room.

What to Do

1. In stalemate situations, make this proposal to the group: "Would you consider resolving this issue by leaving it in the hands of someone we trust and then accepting his or her decision?"

2. If the group agrees, suggest the name of someone who is well regarded. (You should have arranged with this person in advance to serve as mediator if necessary.) Call that person and put him or her on the speaker. First, have one participant lay out the course of action his or her side believes should be pursued. Then, have one participant who's leading the resistance explain his or her position.

3. Have the mediator decide the issue. Thank him or her for helping the group. Then, thank the participants for being willing to move beyond the stalemate. Remind them that, even if the decision was not in their favor, in the long run of their careers, this is not a turning point: they can work to make the outcome beneficial. Therefore, you appreciate their willingness to support the course of action recommended by the outsider.

(If the group doesn't agree to accept the person as mediator, you may need to choose another outsider or try another consensus approach. As a last resort, speak to the individual who seems to be blocking the group's progress. Suggest that if he or she remains vehemently opposed to the proposal, then he or she may wish to consider withdrawing from the group.)

Background/Applications

Even apart from the possibility of hidden agendas, there are numerous reasons why some participants become fixated on having things their own way. Among the things that can get in the way of consensus are:

- differences in experience, background, culture
- misunderstanding of the meeting purpose
- conflicting facts
- widely diverging opinions
- spoken (and unspoken) alignment with certain factions

- tendency to give the issue more importance than it merits
- belief that certain outcomes will benefit an individual or department rather than the organization as a whole.

A group can overcome all of these obstacles, however, when participants commit to using the services of a mediator.

48. *Preventing the Angry Person from Dominating the Discussion*

STORMING THE WAY TO HARMONY

In a Nutshell

One of the best ways to handle anger is to divert it. And this game is a diversionary tactic. With it, you can temporarily stop the flow of vitriol and replace it with a stream of ideas related to storms and the damage they can cause. When you sense some discomfort among meeting members because one or two people are making angry statements, introduce this game as a way of letting people "cool off."

Time

5-10 minutes.

What You'll Need

Flip chart and marking pens; participants will need paper and pens. (Optional: token prizes, such as two umbrellas.)

What to Do

1. Begin by referring to Bruce Tuckman's research on the development of small groups, which consists of four stages: Forming, Storming, Norming, and Performing.

Explain that Storming is a normal part of the success cycle.

2. Then mention that, for a few minutes, you'd like them to think about storms metaphorically. Ask what people do to minimize the possible damage from a storm.

3. Record their answers on the flip chart.

4. Then ask the participants to form pairs to write down the ways those reactions to a storm could be applied to a meeting at which people are Storming. Award token prizes to the pair with the longest list, the pair that volunteers its answers, or the pair with the best answers.

Possible Answers: Minimizing Storm Damage

a. Have a surge-protector to save computer files.
b. Close the windows and doors.
c. Keep candles and matches ready.
d. Bring pets inside.
e. Go to another location.

Possible Answers: Application to the Meeting Process

a. Listen carefully to the person with objections and record all his or her salient points.
b. Close doors during discussion of heated issues so no commotion is caused on the outside.
c. Have soothing music playing in the background when considering an issue likely to raise controversy.
d. Invite a popular figure to serve as mediator.
e. Suggest adjourning to the outdoors for a while.

Background/Applications

Some 40 years ago, Bruce Tuckman created a four-word rhyme to describe the stages of team development: Form, Storm, Norm, and Perform. His extensive research into how teams work led to insights regarding predictable stages—many of which are applicable to teams that convene for a single meeting.

During the Form stage, meeting participants are inevitably concerned about what lies before them. They have many questions, not all of which they're willing to voice. It's imperative for the meeting leader to anticipate and draw out as many questions as possible in order to help team members to function as an integrated whole. A team in the Storm stage must deal with conflicts in perspectives, values, and goals. Surviving this stage depends in very large measure upon the leader's ability to weather the storms, with techniques such as making storm analogies.

During the Norming stage, team members reach consensus regarding how the team will operate and what norms or standards it will maintain and enforce. Finally, having progressed through the first three stages, team members are ready for the Perform stage, to focus on the purpose of the meeting.

49. Determining Content and Context

CAN WE AGREE TO AGREE?

In a Nutshell

Within a matter of seconds, meeting participants (and you) can avoid a possible stalemate by polling to learn where the disagreement really lies—with the *content* of the issue or with the *context* (the process by which the plan would be implemented).

Time

3 minutes.

What You'll Need

Paper and pens for participants.

What to Do

1. Share with meeting participants the fact that decision-makers are often closer to agreement or even unanimity than they realize. It depends on what's dividing them. Some may be objecting to the proposal itself, which is a question of *content*. Others may be reluctant to vote for the

proposal only because they're concerned about the way it would be implemented, which is a question of *context*.

2. Distribute paper and pens and tell participants you'd like them to write just one word on their papers. If they feel the idea or issue itself is *not* worthy of adoption, if they feel it has little value to the organization, if they find fault with the basic premise, they should write, "Content." On the other hand, if they like the idea but think it would be hard to implement or if the context of the idea is difficult or problematic, they should write, "Context." (Of course, if they fully endorse the proposal, they should write nothing.)

3. Ask them fold their papers. Pass an envelope around to collect them.

4. Tally the results. If the majority indicated that the context is the problem, then you should discuss what hurdles the group can overcome. However, if the majority indicated that the idea itself is bad, you may need to direct the discussion toward abandoning the proposal or revamping it for a vote.

Background/Applications

In many ways, when you lead a meeting you must serve as a detective, particularly when meeting participants seem unable to achieve compromise. It's often up to you to root out the underlying causes of disagreement. This game helps you and your group determine if the major obstacle lies with the idea itself or the framework within which it will be executed.

Among the *content* problems might be:

- limited value

- excessive cost

- overly complex

- too long a time required before benefits can be seen

- learning curve too extensive

- too revolutionary for corporate culture.

Among the *context* problems, these are possibilities:

- limited resources

- no champion or advocate for the idea

- poor timing

- turf wars between proposers and implementers

- conflict among the participants

- lack of flexibility regarding implementation.

These, and many other possibilities, offer a starting point for unraveling the mystery that lies behind the reluctance of some participants to support a proposal that seems to have considerable appeal. The guidance you provide as participants ferret out the problems will help them reach consensus.

50. Assessing Futility

Is the Horse Dead Yet?

In a Nutshell

When you sense the discussion is going nowhere, serving no purpose, it's time to introduce this game, designed to give everyone a chance to comment on the discussion. Basically, participants silently indicate whether they'd like to continue or to discontinue the discussion by putting a cartoon drawing in an envelope. The results are counted and the meeting continues.

Time

3 minutes.

What You'll Need

A large envelope; two drawings for each participant: one of an obviously expired horse and the other of a horse that's up and running. (If you can't do simple sketches and don't know anyone who can, buy a book of animal clip art and cut and paste.)

What to Do

1. Diplomatically suggest that the discussion may have run its course, even though participants still have strong feel-

ings about the issue. Suggest an anonymous vote this way: "I'm distributing two drawings now: one of a dead horse, the other of a healthy horse ready to run a few more miles. I'm also going to pass around an envelope. If you feel this discussion is beginning to sound repetitive, please put the dead horse drawing in the envelope when it comes to you. If you think, however, that we might uncover something new that could help break the stalemate, insert the cartoon showing the running horse."

2. Tally the votes in the envelope. If the majority votes to move on, do so, sparing the "chief proponent" the embarrassment of being cut off. If the majority wishes to continue the discussion, set limits on the time to be spent before the group moves on.

Background/Applications

Very often the way you view conflict translates into the way you deal with it. If you regard conflict as a negative, you may attempt to avoid it or respond to it defensively. At least some of the time, others will take their cues from you.

If you can treat conflict in a lighthearted way, as this game does, you can spare the feelings of those participants who feel strongly about a particular point and who show their feelings by talking more and more, hoping to sway others by loquacity if not by logic.

You can't deal with every debated issue in this way, of course. You'll use various techniques in various situations. For more intense discussions, you may want to direct the meeting focus to certain "must-have" outcomes. You may need to emphasize how close you are to the project goal or whether to do a "crash analysis," which explores the application of further resources to the project under way.

Humor works, yes. But not all of the time. The more alternatives you have at your fingertips, the more readily you can find a solution with which the whole group agrees.

51. Employing Persuasion

TELL IT TO THE JUDGE

In a Nutshell

There's both a direct and an indirect purpose to this game. The direct purpose is to achieve consensus by having an outsider vote on the relative merit of two presentations. The indirect purpose is to have a senior management learn how hard the group is working and how seriously the members are taking the work they're doing.

Time

7 minutes.

What You'll Need

A well-respected "outsider" to serve as judge; two tables.

What to Do

1. Tell the group you sense they're clinging to their viewpoints, thus, possibly, making it difficult to achieve consensus. However, you'd like to introduce Mr. or Ms. _____, who has agreed to listen to their "arguments" and rule in favor of one or the other.

2. Divide the group into those who support the proposal

under consideration and those who are opposed to it. (It's possible there might be just one voice on one side or the other. That person will then represent the "pro" or "con" side alone.) Seat the sides at separate tables. Then, give them two minutes to outline a one-minute presentation of their strongest arguments to advance their viewpoint.

3. Have each side make a succinct, one-minute presentation of their rationale.

4. For the remaining two minutes, have the judge explain which position he or she favors and why.

5. Conclude by encouraging the group to adopt the judge's recommendation.

Background/Applications

According to management guru Ken Blanchard, the key to leadership today is *influence*, not authority. This game represents an opportunity for group members to use their persuasion skills in an effort to achieve consensus. Among the tools master persuaders use (and which you may choose to share with the panels) are the following:

- *Cite precedent.* If something is already being done and being done well, examples can considerably diminish any fear of the unknown. This persuasion tool packs a powerful punch.

- *Cite authority.* If a well-respected authority figure, either inside or outside the organization, has endorsed a particular course of action or one similar to it (in theory or in reality), you have a silent partner to plead your cause.

- *Cite statistics.* Putting aside Disraeli's comment that "there are three kinds of lies: lies, damn lies, and statistics," facts and figures can help sway opinion. They must be the right statistics, however, and not too many of them.

- *Ask for a trial period.* If you have complete faith that your proposal will work, one of the best ways to persuade others is to encourage adoption of the proposal for a short time. A trial period doesn't risk much and it allows others to judge the proposal by the results.

■ *Anticipate negative reactions.* Like a good trial attorney, you can steal the thunder of opponents by pointing out the downside of your proposal before they can and then showing how the downside can be minimized.

52. Discovering Underlying Feelings

4 x 4 x 4

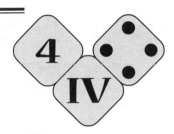

In a Nutshell

This fast-paced game challenges participants to list four ideas on four sheets of paper in only four minutes. A volunteer leaves the room to analyze the ideas. He or she returns to report to the group.

Time

6 minutes.

What You'll Need

A pen and four sheets of paper for each participant.

What to Do

1. Give each participant four sheets of paper. Tell them they'll have to work quickly during the next four minutes. Their assignment: to list one idea on each of four sheets of paper. The ideas should tell how they believe the group could reach consensus on the proposal currently being discussed.

2. Allow them four minutes and then collect the papers. Give them to a volunteer, who will leave the room to analyze

them, looking for frequency of suggestions, unexpected or unusual proposals, strong emotions, etc.

3. Continue with the meeting until the volunteer returns. Then ask for a short report on what he or she learned from the papers and what he or she recommends as the next step.

4. Thank the participants for working as quickly and prolifically as they did. Encourage them to adopt the volunteer's recommendation.

Background/Applications

The human brain, scientists tell us, works at the amazing speed of 800 words, ideas, thoughts, impressions, and/or images a minute. Unfortunately, few meeting leaders tap into this well of intellectual wealth. With this game, you're asking participants for ways to overcome resistance to a proposal. Here are some ways you may wish to deal with this situation:

- Explain that the conflict that's holding the group back from deciding on its next course of action is not necessarily a bad thing. Disagreements usually help ensure that the best solution is found.

- Help participants realize that the conflict is not a battle where one side must defeat the other. Rather, the conflict reflects sincere interest in achieving the best possible solution.

- Remind participants that they can't "win" every time—in meetings and/or in life. If they find themselves conceding today, others will be conceding tomorrow.

- Point out that disputants may be closer to a consensus than they realize. Often, what seem to be diametrically opposed positions are actually similar positions that just need some verbal massaging. Remind them that they should be united by one goal: to determine the best possible outcome for the organization. Keeping the overarching mission in sight can help participants resolve differences.

53. Allocating Assets

SHOW ME THE MONEY!

In a Nutshell

The issue for which you're seeking consensus has to be divided into at least three subdivisions (labeled Parts 1, 2, and 3), which are written on flip chart paper and taped to the wall in advance of the meeting. Participants receive envelopes with one dollar's worth of coins. They indicate with the coins how the group should allocate its time and energy to resolve the issue. (The combinations of coins differ—four quarters, nine dimes and two nickels, and so forth—so participants can make exchanges among themselves so they can allocate their money more exactly.)

Time

5 minutes.

What You'll Need

For each participant, a roll of cellophane tape and an envelope with a dollar's worth of paper coins; flip chart paper, marking pens, and masking tape.

What to Do

1. Explain that one way to work toward consensus is to divide the issue into several parts and have participants vote on the part of the issue they believe is causing dissension in the group.

2. Distribute the envelopes. Ask the participants to "spend" their paper coins by taping them to Parts 1, 2, and 3, allocating their coins according to the degree of difficulty they believe each part is causing the group in terms of reaching consensus.

3. Have a volunteer tally the totals while you explain that the part that collected the largest dollar amount is the one the group will intensely explore.

4. Have the volunteer announce the totals. Then begin the next step in the process: the exploration of the one part that is greater than the whole, as least in terms of causing resistance.

Background/Applications

Stress psychologists tell us that there's only one thing that causes stress—the feeling that we have little or no control over situations. A substantial body of research has grown to support this premise. Low-control working conditions are a leading risk factor contributing to heart disease. Invariably, research has shown that when workers are given some degree of control over their own jobs, they experience less stress and less damage to their hearts. Less stress equates with a happier work environment, which equates with better and more work being done. (Experts estimate that stress costs American organizations $17 billion a year in mistakes, bad decisions, lost time, and lower productivity.)

With this game, you can reduce some of the stress or tension associated with the disagreement barrier. In addition to the benefit of isolating the major factor in the stalemate, this game has a derivative benefit: it gives participants direct control over deciding how to deal with the issue.

54. Using the A–D–D Method

ALL GAIN, NO PAIN

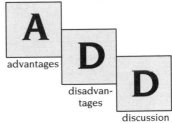

A — advantages

D — disadvantages

D — discussion

In a Nutshell

This pre-vote consensus-builder asks participants to take the issue being debated and consider its advantages, its disadvantages, and the things that need further discussion. The issue is then re-evaluated.

Time

5 minutes.

What You'll Need

Flip chart and marking pens; masking tape; three sheets of paper and a pen for each participant. (Have two sheets of blank chart paper taped to a far wall, one labeled "Advantages" and the other "Disadvantages.")

What to Do

1. Write the topic under discussion on the flip chart. Tell participants they'll have one minute to list advantages, one more to list disadvantages, and a final minute to write things that warrant further discussion. Distribute three sheets of paper to each person as you're explaining this.

Have them write "Advantages" on one, "Disadvantages" on another, and "Discussion" on the third.

2. Give one minute for them to consider advantages of the topic being considered and to write those on the first sheet. Ask a volunteer to collect the papers.

3. Allow another minute for participants to record on the second sheets the disadvantages of the topic for which consensus is being sought. After, ask a second volunteer to collect those papers.

4. For the third minute, have them write down on the third sheet related areas they feel need further debate, discussion, or exploration before a vote can be taken on adopting the idea.

5. Ask the two volunteers to give their Discussion sheets to another participant and write the Advantages and Disadvantages on the flip chart sheets.

6. Record the Discussion points on the flip chart. Call on each person to supply one Discussion point, the one he or she feels is most critical.

7. After one minute, bring closure. If the Discussion list is longer than either of the other two, it's clear the group is not yet ready for the consensus-achieving process. If the Discussion list is relatively short, ask either the Advantages volunteer or the Disadvantages volunteer—whoever had the longer list—to make a report.

Background/Applications

This game affords interesting alternatives:

- Participants can write their thoughts on sheets of chart paper, taped to the wall.

- Participants can work in three groups, one to list advantages, another to list disadvantages, and the third to list points for discussion.

- Participants can discuss each of the three lists over a three-meeting period.

- Participants can vote on whether the longest list should dictate their next action.

The clear benefit of the A-D-D listing is that it brings the issue into focus. If the discussion points are numerous, the group clearly needs much more time for discussion and research before voting. If the advantages of the proposal clearly outweigh the disadvantages, the choice is pretty obvious.

A visual, bar-graphed alternative is the "Five 'L' Straw Poll," proposed by Kristin Arnold, author of *Team Basics*. Using Post-it® notes, participants cast their votes on a continuum: "Loathe" — "Lament" — "Live with" — "Like" — "Love." Consensus is achieved when all the votes fall on the "Live with," "Like," and "Love" end of the continuum.

55. Learning the Strength of Participants' Positions

PROCEED OR SECEDE?

In a Nutshell

On occasion, participants are reluctant to voice their opinions too loudly. Or, if they've already voiced them, they may hesitate to contribute much more, even if they have strong feelings about their position. This game invites a silent statement regarding the intensity of each participant's view of the decision to be made. A second vote is then taken to learn what the group values more: keeping the group intact or achieving consensus.

Time

4 minutes.

What You'll Need

A pen and three sheets of paper for each participant.

What to Do

1. When it seems the group has reached an impasse, try this game to find out how strongly all participants feel about their positions. Announce you'd like everyone to make a

choice. Do they feel that they can go ahead no matter what concessions would have to be made so consensus can be achieved? If so, they'll write the word "Proceed" on a sheet of paper. Or do they feel so strongly about their position that they would prefer to resign rather than accept an "I can live with it" result? In that case, they should write the word "Recede."

2. Collect and tally the votes. If you have all "Proceed" votes, it's clear the group is bent on working on a decision in which everyone wins. If you have any "Recede" votes, however, explain that one or more participants apparently feel so strongly about a position or positions—and it could be a "pro" position or a "con" position, a majority position or a minority position—that he, she, or they would be willing to leave the group rather than endorse a compromise position.

3. Ask the group to vote once more. This time, though, you'll ask them which is more important to them: to keep the group intact or to achieve consensus. They'll write either "Intact" or "Consensus" on their sheets.

4. Again, tally the votes and address the situation as follows.

5. If all members of the group wrote "Intact," they're telling you they believe a consensus is possible and are willing to give up a little in order to achieve an outcome that's acceptable to the group.

6. If you had one or more "Consensus" votes, however, you're putting the group on notice that, unless a workable solution can be reached, the group integrity may be broken. Announce that there will be a short break before you take the consensus poll. Affirm your wish to keep the group intact, but say you understand the strength of conviction. If the vote is one that someone cannot live with, afford him or her the opportunity to quietly leave the room and leave the group during the break.

Background/Applications

One of your goals as meeting leader has to be to not waste time—especially in view of the statistics regarding meetings: the time any of us spends in meetings throughout our careers would total several years. To ensure productivity, you need to plumb the depth of participants' feelings, particularly when the issue under consideration is controversial.

With this game, you can learn not only how strongly individuals feel but also how strongly the group feels about its structural integrity.

The Social Judgment Theory, espoused by Carolyn W. Sherif in *Attitude and Attitude Change*, alludes to the importance of allowing participants to voice their positions and then to withdraw from the group if their values prevent them from endorsing a given decision.

This theory discusses a continuum. The first part covers the "latitude of acceptance." Here you'll find participants leaning toward accepting the proposal. In the middle is the "latitude of noncommitment." In this middle range are the participants who have not made up their minds one way or the other. At the other end of the continuum is the "latitude of rejection," in which participants are taking a firm, possibly unmovable position. If they absolutely refuse to budge, there are only two ways out of the stalemate: reject the proposal altogether and start anew or "reject" the participant (in the most diplomatic, gracious way possible) from the group. The very fact, though, that anyone may be willing to sacrifice group membership should give the group pause: if he or she feels this strongly, they may be a danger to the organization that the group has been overlooking.

Part Seven

ENGAGING AND ENERGIZING MEETING PARTICIPANTS

Ironically, it's altogether possible that the participant who least wishes to be in the meeting may well be one of the most conscientious employees in the organization. That's because many separate meetings from "work." They worry about the work not getting done while they're in a meeting instead of believing that the meeting is their work.

Unfortunately, this belief is just one of the challenges facing the meeting leader. There are uncountable other reasons why participants may be disengaged or enervated. The games that follow provide numerous possibilities for taking limited interest to interesting limits.

In "Exerting Control in Meetings," participants are actively involved in listing the causes of any current malaise. Then, they're asked to take charge, to honestly determine which of those causes they can actually do something about.
In the second game, participants are introduced to Walter Shewhart and his famous cycle; then they're asked to develop a cycle of their own. The "hands-on" nature of the games in this section continues with "Developing a Meeting Charter,"

which has participants determine what elements should be in that charter. (The rules of engagement in this game have participants providing feedback numerous times in the course of the game.)

The next game has participants shouting out answers to a brainteaser that requires a sense of the big picture. It provides the perfect segue into a discussion of the dangers of making assumptions or looking at a situation too narrowly, too literally. Participants have a chance to develop their meeting communications in the fifth game, as they list meeting-related words and discuss them.

The focus of the next game is Peter Drucker's comment that leaders know how to ask the right questions, but with a twist: it invites participants to ask the questions of the meeting leader. With a very challenging exercise in the following game, participants learn how well they can concentrate, a valuable skill both in meetings and outside. (The game allows you to use words that emphasize meeting goals, if you wish.)

It's important to have a balance of behaviors in meetings and the eighth game, "Assessing Task and Maintenance Behaviors," helps assess the range of meeting behaviors. Finally, in "Preparing a Meeting Timeline," participants begin with an energizer akin to the qualifying round in the TV show, *Who Wants to Be a Millionaire?* From there, they work on a timeline germane to the meeting purpose.

56. Exerting Control in Meetings

SUBJUGATING STRESS

In a Nutshell

When meeting participants are discouraged, dejected, dispirited, this game can provide a quick emotional pickup. It's based on stress research regarding *external* versus *internal* control. Participants can see how much control they actually have by listing the sources of concern and then writing the letter C in front of those over which they have full or partial control.

Time

5 minutes.

What You'll Need

Flip chart and marking pens.

What to Do

1. Begin by pointing out that meeting participants sometimes feel discouraged when they feel they're not getting anywhere or when they feel they have less power than the powers that be. They may feel frustrated and then apathetic if it seems all decisions are made by others, as if all considerations are beyond their control. Assure them

that, in fact, they can exert considerable power over the outcomes of their own meetings. Then ask them to think about the things that are getting them down.

2. Have them shout out the sources of stress or concern or worry. Record them on the flip chart.

3. Then, item by item, ask, "Is this something over which we can exert some control?" If so, preferably with a neon marker, write the letter "C" beside each item. (If not, leave the item untouched.)

4. Participants will soon see that they can, in fact, improve their circumstances if they choose to do so.

Background/Applications

As a little experiment, you may wish to ask your meeting participants, "How do you know when you've done a good job?" Don't call on volunteers to answer, because the "wrong" answer could be embarrassing. Treat it as a rhetorical question. Simply point out that if someone answered, "I know it's good when my boss compliments me on it," chances are that person has a low personal-control factor. He or she is dependent on others for approval or is relying too much on external-control factors. On the other hand, those with answers like "I know it's good when it meets my standards" have internal-control factors; that suggests an empowered status.

Another way to regard the question is to ask participants to think of all the things they do on a weekly basis. Then ask how many of those they're doing because they want to be doing them and how many they're doing because others expect or want those things done. Ask participants to express their answers as a percentage, such as "30% my choice, 70% others' demands." The higher the "my choice" percentage, the healthier the person's psychological state.

It's true that if we work for someone else, then we have to do what's asked of us. But this doesn't mean the internal-control percentage has to be low. First, ideally at least, the person is in that job because he or she wants to be. By extension, he or she wants to be doing what is asked. Second, many empowered employees work quasi-independently, with a low external-control factor.

Bring the discussion around to meetings. Ideally, you're presenting your participants with numerous choices, in order to limit the external control that is exerted by an autocratic meeting leader or in an organization that expects its people to meet its demands without discussion.

57. Employing the P–D–C–A Cycle

SHEWHART'S SHOW

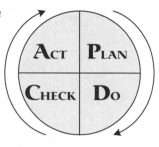

In a Nutshell

The famous Shewhart Cycle (P-D-C-A) is presented as an overall scheme for the way team members work to achieve their goals. For meetings that are not team meetings, but rather one-time gatherings of like-minded people to make a decision or solve a problem, a microcosmic version of the Shewhart Cycle will be developed.

Time

5-7 minutes.

What You'll Need

Overhead projector; several roles of cellophane tape; one sheet of typing paper for each pair of participants; token prizes; one pair of scissors for each pair of participants; three copies of Handout (page 175) for each pair. (If possible, four blank wooden cubes measuring 1½ inches across, found in any crafts store. If you use the cubes, supply each pair of participants with a permanent marking pen. The other materials are then unnecessary, except for the token prizes.)

What to Do

1. Begin with a brief mention of Walter Shewhart, whose work led to many of the quality principles so popular in the 1980s. Explain that his cycle of Planning, Doing, Checking, and Acting is most appropriate for implementing a new procedure or process. (If the participants will be meeting for a long-term assignment, discuss at this point how their efforts will conform to the general guidelines established by Shewhart.) Then note that a singular meeting can be viewed as a microcosmic reflection of that macrocosmic cycle.

2. Have the participants form pairs. Then ask them to come up with a formula of their own, to lay out the process they believe the meeting cycle should undergo, either cutting letters from the handouts and taping them to the typing paper or using the markers and the blocks. (An example might be B-P-S-S, standing for Brainstorm-Prioritize-Select-Summarize, depending on the meeting purpose.)

3. Ask each pair to briefly tell what their letters stand for in reference to the process that meeting members should use to achieve their goal.

4. Then have the whole group decide on the most efficient cycle and award token prizes to the winning pair.

Background/Applications

Walter Shewhart's PDCA (Plan-Do-Check-Act) approach to improvement, later modified by W. Edwards Deming as PDSA (Plan-Do-Study-Act), applies to the improvement of any process, including the process of team meetings. The agenda that the team leader prepares (and, ideally, sends out ahead of time) reflects the Plan step. The meeting itself reflects the Do step, the execution of the plan. The leader must then Check to determine the success of the plan.

Typically, team leaders don't do such checking. But this evaluation need not be complex or time-consuming. It can be done formally or informally, orally or in writing, by team members or by an outsider. But, periodically, groups should make assessments and take Action (the "A" part of the Shewhart Cycle) to improve, based on they learned during the Check stage.

On a larger scale, the Shewhart Cycle can be used for managing processes. For a broad-scope project, the Plan stage will require more than one meeting, as will the other stages. Of course, other letters can be used to describe how a given meeting should progress. The cycle ideas suggested by participants will no doubt rival Shewhart's Cycle in their logical flow and comprehensiveness. (If the cubes are used, a transition can easily be made to the need for building a "foundation" for action.)

Shewhart's Show

A   B   C   D   E

F   G   H   I   J   K

L   M   N   O   P

Q   R   S   T   U   V

W   X   Y   Z

58. Developing a Meeting Charter

CHARTERING YOUR COURSE

In a Nutshell

This game asks triads to list the truly important elements of a charter for a group that will be having several future meetings to achieve its goal. Each pair presents its list; the remaining pairs vote on the number of insignificant topics that were mentioned.

Time

5-7 minutes.

What You'll Need

Flip chart and marking pens; participants will need paper and pens; small sheets of paper for voting—enough so each participant has one for half the number of participants present. (In a meeting with eight participants, for example, each participant would receive four small sheets.) (Optional: token prizes.)

What to Do

1. Briefly discuss the differences between the charter, which offers a guide for achieving long-term goals, and the ground rules, which govern individual behavior.

2. Have participants form pairs, to brainstorm topics that should be addressed in a charter. The items listed should be meaningful, ones that are truly worth the group's consideration.

3. Have each pair report on its results. Call on one member of each pair to read its list. Have the other pairs write on a sheet of paper the number of topics (if any) they feel are not important enough to include in a charter. Collect the votes and give them to the pair reporting.

4. The pair with the lowest total of unimportant items wins.

Background/Applications

One common factor in the meeting-success equation is the formulation of a charter—a clearly written agreement that covers such elements as mission, outcomes, boundaries, customer expectations, voting procedures, duties, authority, resources, role of the sponsors, progress reports, etc. The charter is especially useful for groups that anticipate meeting several times before achieving their goal. The charter differs from ground rules, which basically cover team members' behavior. The charter, by contrast, is a deeper and broader determination of operating principles.

A peripheral benefit of this game is the introduction of a voting tool that is quick and easy and spares participants' feelings. When several suggestions or proposals are up for a vote, the meeting leader has participants make their choice on slips of paper, collects them, puts them in an envelope, and then tallies the votes during a break. The leader can then simply announce the winning idea and the person(s) who proposed it.

59. Encouraging Beyond-the-Obvious Thinking

JAIL TALE

In a Nutshell

This game is a good prelude to setting the stage for defining a problem. Participants are asked to solve a puzzle. Then, they discuss the danger of assumptions. Finally, they examine some of the assumptions that may surround their meeting purpose.

Time

5 minutes.

What You'll Need

Flip chart and marking pens; participants will need paper and pens. (Optional: prize for the first person to figure out the puzzle.)

What to Do

1. Read the following story to the meeting participants: "This is the tale of a man who got out of jail. The first thing he did was push a car to a nearby hotel. Then he left a large amount of money there. His next action was

similar: he pushed the car to a house in the area and left money there, too, although less money than he'd left at the hotel. Can you explain what's going on here?"

2. Elicit answers, which will be numerous and obvious, but the prize will go to the person who realizes the description pertains to a player using the Monopoly game board.

3. Award the prize (or applause at least) to the first person to demonstrate outside-the-box thinking. Then briefly discuss the dangers of assumptions and of interpretations that are too broad or too narrow.

Background/Applications

Meeting members often place unnecessary restrictions on themselves. By narrowing the boundaries within which they are free to operate, they make their job more difficult. The reverse is true as well. Teams sometimes decide their task is bigger and/or their freedoms are greater than they really are. It's the meeting leader's role to clear up preconceptions and misconceptions. The following questions will help:

- What barriers do we face?
- What do you/we need to know?
- What boundaries constrain us?
- What are we free to do?
- What's the reward for success?
- Is there a penalty for success?
- What's the price of failure?
- Is there any reward for failure?
- How will voting be conducted?
- When should "outsiders" be invited to attend our meetings?
- What roles will members have to play?

- What expectations do you have for the team leader?

- What is expected of us?

- What do you expect of us?

- What resources are available to us?

- How much time will be required of us?

- What's in it for us?

- What happens when we meet our goal?

You can also discuss the pros and cons of having a bird's eye view of a situation—overarching, visionary, strategic, comprehensive—or a worm's eye view of it—focused, detailed, analytical, quantitative. Point out that both viewpoints are valuable. What's dangerous is to use only one and not the other. Again, it's important to have a meeting participants who reflect diversity—of cultures, thinking styles, positions, backgrounds, experience, gender, age, and so on. Diversity helps avoid groupthink tendencies.

60. Improving Meeting Communication

ALPHABET SOUP OF MEETINGS

In a Nutshell

Using a transparency to expedite thinking, meeting participants will free—associate words related to meetings in general or, in particular, to the purpose of the meeting they're
attending now.

Time

5—10 minutes.

What You'll Need

Overhead projector; Transparency (page 184); flip chart and
marking pens; participants will need paper and pens; five
token prizes.

What to Do

1. Have participants write their names on their papers. Show
   the transparency. Ask participants to quickly free-associate, to select any letter and use it as the first letter of a
   word—good, bad, or ugly—that they usually associate
   with meetings.

2. Have them do the same with as many letters as possible, writing as many words as possible. If they like, they can use one letter and spin several words from it, but each word must start with that letter. Tell them not to think too deeply about their selection, just to free-associate from as many letters to as many words as possible. All the words must be related to meetings.

3. Collect the papers and ask two people to be judges. With the papers spread out before them, they will quickly scan to determine who wins the token prizes, using the following criteria:
   - Who has the longest list of words?
   - Who has the most interesting word?
   - Who has the most negative word?
   - Who has the most positive word?
   - Who has the funniest word?

4. Write the names of the five people and their winning answers on the flip chart. Then lead a motivational discussion reviewing meeting expectations.

5. You can extend the activity by asking questions such as these:
   - In the alphabet soup of meetings, which letter (and corresponding words) do you choke on?
   - Which letter (and word) goes down smoothly?
   - Which letter (and word) is too hot to swallow?
   - Which letter (and word) is cold to the taste?

Background/Applications

Some of America's best management minds are the most critical of meetings. "One either meets or one works. One cannot do both at the same time," Peter Drucker once commented, suggesting that no work is done at meetings. He also said that if a manager spends more than 25% of his or her time in meetings it's a sign of malorganization. Anonymous commentators have made the following comments: "If an hour has been spent amending a sentence, someone will move to delete the paragraph," "Too many meetings are held each month for no better reason than it has been a month since the last one," and "The length of a meeting rises with the square of the number of people present." Robert Half, of executive search firm fame, notes, "America leads the world not in steel or textiles but in meetings. The problem is, how do you export meetings?"

It's no secret that many people regard meetings as a waste of time. If you are to assure the members of the team that your meetings will be different, you need to address their concerns. And freely associated words provide an excellent means of uncovering just what those concerns are. Invite the five prize-winners to share their thoughts:

- *Longest number of words.* Ask the winner if he or she has had extensive meeting experience (perhaps explaining why the list was so long). Then ask about the most valuable lesson the person has learned from all that experience.

- *Most interesting word.* Ask the winner why he or she selected the word and how it might relate to the purpose of the current meeting.

- *Most negative word.* Briefly discuss with the winner ways to make sure that the current meeting doesn't merit that label.

- *Most positive word.* Ask the winner for input on how to replicate the positive aspects of successful meetings in the current meeting.

- *Funniest word.* Point out that successful meetings always have a moment or two of levity. Ask this winner if you can call upon him or her to provide such at the current and future meetings.

Alphabet Soup of Meetings

A   B   C   D   E

F   G   H   I   J   K

L   M   N   O   P

Q   R   S   T   U   V

W   X   Y   Z

61. Following Drucker's Advice for Leaders

ASKING THE RIGHT QUESTIONS

In a Nutshell

The purpose of this game is to energize meeting participants by giving them an opportunity to ask questions of the meeting leader. The game provides a quick energizer and, usually, a lot of laughter for recharging drained batteries.

Time

5 minutes.

What You'll Need

Paper and pens for participants.

What to Do

1. Cite Peter Drucker and mention what he had to say about leadership: "Leaders know how to ask questions, the right questions." Say that, as their meeting leader, you have what you believe to be a right question for them. And that question is "What questions do you have for me?"

2. Ask each person to write one meeting-related question

that you promise to answer. Have fold up their papers and toss them into the center of the table.

3. Take the questions, one by one, and answer them—even those that may sound like an attack. For example, you could answer the question "Don't you ever come up for air?" with a bit of humor: "My wife tells me I'm never at a loss for words but always at a loss for funds. But, on the basis of this question, I promise to talk less and listen more."

Background/Applications

It's not just Drucker who offers interesting insights about the questioning process. Here are additional views that apply to the meeting process.

By the judicious use of questions, you can easily secure immediate attention, maintain interest in the item under discussion, and direct the course that you want the conversation to take.

—Gerard I. Nierenberg,
Founder of the Negotiation Institute

Consider making a tape recording of your meetings and playing it back when you're alone. How many questions do you ask? How judiciously? How well do they gain the group's attention? How well do they maintain focus on the discussion? How well do they direct the discussion? If you're dissatisfied with the results, work on improving your questioning and make another tape several weeks later.

It is better to know some of the questions than all of the answers.

—James Thurber, *The Thurber Carnival*

As contrarian as this viewpoint might be, the truth is we live in an age of paradox, when oxymoronic ideas sometimes have merit. This quotation reminds us that we don't have to have answers—at least not immediately—to every question that's posed. Devise some questions that you'd like to leave hanging, so they can cause a kind of creative tension. In other words, participants will ruminate about these (especially if they're prominently posted in the meeting room) and will return to them until they've resolved the mental tension.

> The way you ask a question has a lot to do with the answer you get.
>
> —Glenn Varney, professor emeritus of management, Bowling Green State University, and organization development expert

What makes a good question, one that's more likely to get good answers? Syntax is important, of course. But so are frequency, time, place, tone, and audience, and relevancy.

There's truly an art to being a good questioner, as detectives, attorneys, and interviewers can attest. If you're serious about improving your facilitation skills, you'll do well to attend to your questioning abilities.

62. Improving Concentration Skills

SIGHTING LIKE CATS AND DOGS

In a Nutshell

In this game, participants will have a chance to think about the key meeting issues while simultaneously (and paradoxically) taking a mental break. They have to "decipher" words that have been broken up letter by letter. Indirectly, they'll be reminded of the team purpose as well.

Time

3-5 minutes.

What You'll Need

A handout; flip chart and marking pens; paper and pens for participants. (Optional: a token prize for the winner.)

What to Do

1. In advance of the meeting, prepare the handout. Think of at least 10 six-letter words that pertain to the meeting purpose or project. (Seven- or eight-letter words, like those in the sample, are even better.)

   Type the words in a large, easy-to-read font like this for the words "contract" and "facility":

[c f] [o a] [n c] [t i] [r l] [a i] [c t] [t y]

Each line on the handout will consist of two words split up. There will be five lines, at least, so that the handout presents at a minimum of 10 words.

2. Tell participants, "You deserve a break today, a mental break. And I have just what you need. There'll be a prize for the first person to figure out the words on the handout. They're all familiar words and all relate to what we've been doing in this meeting. However, the words are written in an unusual way. Here's what I mean. If I wrote 'cat' as '[c] [a] [t],' you'd have no trouble recognizing it. And if I wrote 'dog' as '[d] [o] [g],' you'd get the word immediately. But if I alternated the letters of the two words, it would be a lot harder: '[d c] [o a] [g t].' The words on the handout have been written like that. Who can figure out all of them first?"

3. Distribute the handout. Award a prize to the first person to figure out all of the words. Ask him or her which word he or she believes is most critical to meeting success.

Background/Applications

You might not think there's a relationship between the ability to concentrate and the degree of participation. But Ralph Erber, associate professor of psychology at DePaul University, noted 20 years ago, in an interview with *Working Woman*, "When you do something that requires all your concentration, there is little room for other thoughts—including depressing ones." In a study of moods, researchers showed movies with sad outcomes to 112 people, in an attempt to cause temporary depression. The researchers then tasked them with working on a challenging assignment. Those who worked the hardest and contributed the most afterwards reported feeling more upbeat and optimistic than those who made little or no effort to become involved.

In your role as meeting leader, you'll sometimes have to deliberately inject humor into a meeting when participants are less than engaged or energized. But you can also change the mood of a meeting by getting the participants to concentrate on a task.

63. Assessing Task and Maintenance Behaviors

ARE YOU TASK'D TO THE MAX?

In a Nutshell

The purpose of this quick game is to learn the orientation of meeting participants: are they more *task*-oriented or more *maintenance*-oriented? You'll wind up the game by stressing the importance of having both behaviors operative at meetings.

Time

3 minutes.

What You'll Need

A small piece of paper for each participant and a pen; a large envelope.

What to Do

1. Review the difference between task and maintenance behaviors. *Task* behaviors help to accomplish the task; they would be things like asking for clarification, monitoring time, reminding the group of purpose, asking others to pay attention, offering suggestions, serving as recorder,

191

etc. *Maintenance* behaviors can be regarded as the social glue that holds the group together; when you compliment someone, thank someone, inquire about their health, or offer to get something for them, you are helping to maintain a high level of interpersonal exchanges. Maintenance-oriented individuals are "people" people. Yes, the work they have to do is important to them—but equally important are the feelings of those doing the work.

2. Explain that you'd like to get a sense of how the members of the group view themselves. Are they primarily task-oriented? If so, they should write "T" on the paper. If they're more inclined toward Maintenance behaviors, they should write "M."

3. Collect the papers, count the T's and M's into two piles, and share the results with the group.

4. Remind them of the importance of having both types of behavior in effect at every meeting—and also the importance of *being* both types. Each participant has an obligation to engage in both task and maintenance behaviors as called for.

Background/Applications

You may choose to provide a fuller description of the two types of behaviors.

Task behaviors include the following:

■ *Redirecting.* When the discussion is deviating from the posted agenda, when war stories become too detailed, when one person has been on center stage too long, the task-oriented participant (or meeting leader) will redirect the group to the mission or purpose of the meeting.

■ *Probing.* When the issue is not clear, when quieter members have not been contributing, when reactions are needed, probing behavior is needed. Basically, it puts a temporary halt to the proceedings by ensuring there is understanding before next steps are taken.

- *Initiating.* When a volunteer is needed, when a stalemate has occurred, when silence spreads over the group, when participants appear "brain-dead," the initiator suggests a new course of action.

Maintenance behaviors include the following:

- *Reconciling.* When an abrasive word has been spoken, when trouble appears to be brewing between two participants, when there's an impasse, when someone's been verbally attacked, the maintenance-skilled participant will step in to smooth things over and restore a sense of harmony.

- *Socializing.* When the meeting has not yet started, when humor is called for, when participants need to know each other a little better, when the group has completed an especially difficult task, when the group needs a mental break—all of these are times when the emphasis can switch from "getting the job done" to "keeping the job doers happy."

- *Praising.* When an individual has gone out of his or her way for the meeting participants or has done an exceptional job related to the mission, when the group has succeeded at something, when outside feedback has been channeled through the meeting leader, when the group has agreed to go beyond what was asked of it—the need for praise will arise several times during a meeting. Be careful, though, that your praise is sincere and specific, not the one-comment-fits-all-situations generic type that's virtually meaningless.

You may also choose to appoint a "shadow" from among the meeting participants or—better still—from outside the group. His or her job will be to observe the meeting to learn if there's a balance of the two types of behaviors or if the group as a whole needs to evince more of one type. The shadow could also observe the behaviors of a given participant to learn about his or her pattern. To avoid making it seem that any one person is being isolated, the shadow would have to observe each person (one at a time) over the course of the meeting or over several meetings.

64. Preparing a Meeting Timeline

Is That Your Final Answer?

In a Nutshell

Like the qualifying round in the popular television show, *Who Wants to Be a Millionaire?*, this game first asks participants to prepare a timeline based on national events. Then, you'll ask them to prepare a timeline as a group, depicting important events or occurrences in relation to the work they have before them. (Some of these events, of course, will project into the future.)

Time

6 minutes.

What You'll Need

Overhead projector; Transparency (page 198); several sheets of flip chart paper, taped together along the wall prior to the start of the meeting; masking tape; marking pens; participants will need paper and pens. (Optional: token prize, such as an old history book.)

What to Do

1. Begin with a challenge. Show Transparency and say, "You

have exactly one minute to place these national events in chronological order, starting with the earliest and progressing to the most current.

a. The United States entered World War II.
b. The North American Free Trade Agreement was passed.
c. The minimum wage was set by President Kennedy at $1.25 an hour.
d. Congress passed the Occupational Safety and Health Act.
e. The Fair Labor Standards Act was passed to establish the 40-hour work week."

2. Award the token prize to the first person who places the events in this order: e, a, c, d, b. (If anyone is interested, the corresponding years are 1938, 1941, 1961, 1970, 1983.)

3. Then ask, "What are some of the key organizational events that have impacted and are impacting the meeting purpose?" Discuss what participants propose for two minutes. Ask them to think, too, about the times associated with goal achievement.

4. Distribute marking pens and, for the remaining three minutes, have participants prepare a meeting timeline, using the chart paper on the wall.

5. Circulate among them as they do so, reminding them of how far they've come and how close they are to their goal.

Background/Applications

Timelines such as the one created in this game help meeting members gain a broader perspective on their task, how far they've come in accomplishing it, and how far they have yet to go.

If a group meets over an extended time, it's important to periodically assess its progress with timelines. In the discussion that accompanies doing the timeline, you should revisit certain questions pertinent to goal achievement. For example:

- Has our goal shifted?

- Has our customer added or subtracted any needs?

- Do we still have the resources we need?

- Will we be able to meet our deadline?

- What evidence do we have that we're on the right track?

- Do we need additional people in our meetings?

- What assurances do we have that our outcomes will be accepted?

Timeline

Starting with the earliest and progressing to the most current, list these events in order.

a. The United States entered World War II.

b. The North American Free Trade Agreement was passed.

c. The minimum wage was set by President Kennedy at $1.25 hour.

d. Congress passed the Occupational Safety and Health Act.

e. The Fair Labor Standards Act was passed to establish the 40-hour work week.

Part Eight

Making Group Decisions

It's not uncommon for groups that function well in every other meeting capacity to halt their progress when it comes to making a decision. That's where you come in: there are any number of tactics you can employ to help groups escape decision-paralysis. For openers, you can do the following:

- *Establish a climate of receptivity.* Advise the group that decisions are merely steppingstones on the path to closure. They are almost never life-or-death turning points. Acknowledge that not all decisions will be popular with all participants. However, unless decisions are made, the group will simply not be able to advance. When the group is about to consider options, state that many or all of them have merit and that options that are not selected won't necessarily be forgotten. The options not chosen can be placed in the "parking lot"—a sheet of flip chart paper for items to be reviewed at a later time by these or other meeting participants.

- *Establish a framework for the decisions.* Not all decisions can or should be made by the whole group. Some should be made by the meeting leader, some by the leader with input from others, some by the leader as merely one of the voting participants, and some by the voting participants alone. Discuss ahead of time what types of decisions will be made, by whom, and by what voting method.

- ■ *Establish understanding of the decision-making process.* Although techniques will differ, as shown in the games that follow, the process basically remains the same. There must be an input. There must be an output. And in between there must be steps during which participants express their thoughts about the decisions to be made.

The first game uses the multi-voting process, which helps participants reach a decision by voting several times and then allowing the majority to rule for the final, reduced list of two or three choices. Another effective tool is presented in the next game, the BeWoLi approach, which brings participants closer to a decision by asking them to consider the best, worst, and most likely outcomes. The third game, "Applying a Morphological Analysis," uses a highly interactive process that calls for some morphing of the prospect being considered.

The next game features the decision tree, a visual delineation of the various aspects of the situation that calls for a vote. From ancient Greece comes the Delphi technique; in the fifth game it's used to invite honest but anonymous feedback on the issue participants are studying, prior to a vote. With the sixth game, participants use the nominal group process to reach a decision that is based on both the number of votes and the relative priorities assigned to each choice.

In the seventh game in this section, "Conducting a System Analysis," participants employ impressions, facts, analysis, and planning to reach their decisions. The final game presents comparative valuation, a tool that should be used for making major, strategic decisions.

65. *Using Multi-Voting*

NOTE THE VOTE

In a Nutshell

Some interesting dynamics will pop up as participants play this game, designed to reduce the number of choices to be considered before a final vote. To begin, two groups list names of possible conference keynoters. Then, the whole group multi-votes to reduce the list. The fun here lies in the unwritten rules.

Time

15 minutes.

What You'll Need

Red, yellow, and blue circular adhesive stickers, about 1 inch in diameter (one of each color for each participant); flip chart and marking pens.

What to Do

1. Divide the group in half. Ask each team to come up with a flip chart list of at least 10 names of keynote speakers for an upcoming conference on racial and gender diversity. Participants are to assume money is no object. Have

them work quietly so the other team doesn't hear their choices or send one team to a break-out room.

[Note: Because it's a conference on racial and gender diversity, participants should be listing names like Colin Powell, Secretary of State; Elaine Chao, Secretary of Labor; Wilma Mankiller, former chief of the Cherokee Nation; and Melvin Martinez, Secretary of Housing and Urban Development.]

2. When the teams return, have them post their lists. You'll thank them as you mark a bright "+1" in front of the names of any persons who are not white males. Determine which team won the game and explain why.

3. Proceed to the multi-voting stage. Write the names (eliminating duplicates) on a single sheet of chart paper. Explain that multi-voting is a series of votes to reduce the number of choices and that it begins with a list of 20 or more possibilities. Meeting participants vote on one-third of the possibilities each time.

4. Ask participants to choose, individually, seven names from the list and write them on a sheet of paper. These are their preferences; they don't have to prioritize them.

5. Tally the votes and write the number of votes next to each name on the original two chart-paper lists.

6. Cross off those names that earned no, one, or two votes.

7. Ask participants to vote again on one-third of the remaining number.

8. Tally and record the votes, using a marking pen of a different color.

9. Continue in this way until you've reduced the list to two or three names.

10. Now have participants, one at a time, walk up to the flip chart and place their red sticker on their top choice, the yellow sticker on their second-favorite choice, and—if

there are three names—the blue sticker on their third-favorite choice. The name with the most red stickers is the final choice.

Background/Applications

With truly important votes that warrant the investment of voting time, the multi-voting procedure works well. Unlike a quick show of hands, which allows for the majority to rule, the multi-voting allows participants a greater control over outcomes by inviting their input on more than one set of choices.

There are a few things to remember when conducting a multi-voting session:

- Don't use it in lieu of "majority rules" votes. Some decisions simply do not require this investment of time.

- Make certain the original list has at least 20 choices. If the total is not readily divisible by three, round up to a number divisible by three to calculate one-third. For example, if there are 20 choices, round up to 21 and ask participants to vote on seven of the possibilities.

- Make certain the lists are printed as neatly as possible, since the cross-outs and numbers can make the lists hard to read.

- Use different colors of marking pens to make the lists easier to read.

- If voting reduces your final list to only two choices, you can simply vote by a show of hands. However, if you sense participants need a stretch break at this time, you can have them walk up to the list and vote with their stickers.

- Some meeting leaders, if there are but two choices left, will postpone a final decision until outside advice can be sought. The final two may each be worthy of pursuing. It may be possible to do both. If not, you may want to let someone in senior management weigh in with his or her opinion.

66. Determining Best, Worst, and Most Likely Outcomes

BEDAZZLE WITH BEWOLI

In a Nutshell

This simple but effective tool has meeting participants look at best possible outcomes, worst possible outcomes, and most likely outcomes for several choices that will be put to a vote. The purpose of using this tool is to show at a glance which option looks most promising, thus facilitating decision-making. The process works best whenever the group has two or more significant choices.

Time

5 minutes.

What You'll Need

Flip chart and marking pens; masking tape; participants will need paper and pens.

What to Do

1. Cite the benefit of stepping back from a situation from time to time and examining the broader scope or the bigger context for the problem to be solved. Ask if the group

is willing to go with a majority-rules vote on the alternatives they've been studying.

2. If so, divide the participants into groups, one for each alternative. On the flip chart, write the alternatives under consideration. Assign an alternative to each group.

3. Ask each group to consider its assigned alternative and to project the best possible outcomes, the worst possible outcomes, and the most realistic outcomes on a sheet of chart paper, which the group will later tape to the wall.

4. After three minutes, ask participants to stand and study the outcomes listed for each of the alternatives and then to mark a star on the one alternative they feel represents the group's best choice.

5. Announce the decision.

Background/Applications

Although some meeting groups talk off-the-cuff about decisions and then make seat-of-the-pants choices, other groups prefer a more analytical approach. The more analytical approach usually yields a better outcome. Yes, the analysis can include intuitive thinking—the feelings that participants have about the choices and the decision-making process—but the rational mode offers meeting participants a sense of security, for it's concrete, discernable, and based on logic.

The urgency of the situation, important issues, the people and things that will be impacted—participants must take all of these factors into consideration as they consider best outcomes, worst outcomes, and most likely outcomes. The best possible scenario should also specify the "musts" and the "wants," i.e., requirements and benefits that will derive from a given decision. In exploring the worst outcomes, decision-makers have to pay attention to possible obstacles as well as the negative consequences that could result. And, in looking at the most likely outcomes, participants consider all of the realities of the situation, the existing facts, figures, personalities, culture, climate, etc.

67. Applying a Morphological Analysis

MORPH! DON'T DWARF!

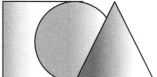

In a Nutshell

This quick and loud adaptation of a morphological analysis requires one honest person to be a listening judge. He or she stands in the front of the room and decides on the best alternative based on the volume of affirmations each alternative receives. The shouted responses are prompted by questions you'll ask about each alternative.

Time

5 minutes.

What You'll Need

Flip chart and marking pens; masking tape. (Optional: a pair of earplugs as a gift of appreciation for the judge.) (Caution: This game works best in a room that's somewhat isolated, for the noise level will definitely rise above the normal. You may consider going outside for these five minutes.)

What to Do

1. Write on the flip chart the remaining alternatives—two is best, three at the most—that are under consideration. List the two primary benefits of each alternative.

2. Tape the alternatives and their two benefits to the wall, so they're clearly visible.

3. On a second sheet of flip chart paper, record the answers the group gives to these three questions:
   - Who will be affected by our decision today?
   - Who will benefit by it, directly or indirectly?
   - Who has a stake in our decision or an interest in it?

   Aim for a list of five names of individuals or groups.

4. Ask for a volunteer to be the listening judge. He or she will come to the front of the room and stand facing the wall, so he or she can make a judgment solely on the basis of sound. Give him or her a pad and pencil and suggest making notes during the voting process.

5. Begin with the first benefit of the first alternative. Quickly read the name of the first person or group on the list. Ask the group to show with their voices the degree to which that person or group would appreciate or approve benefit #1 of alternative #1. Move on to the other names on the list, pausing briefly after each so that group can indicate by volume the importance of the alternative to each of the individuals or groups listed.

6. Do the same thing with the second benefit of the first alternative: ask the participants to assess the benefit in terms of each name on the list, one by one.

7. Move on to the second alternative, using the same procedure as for the first.

8. If there are three alternatives, follow the same procedure for the third.

9. Ask the judge for his or her decision. Thank him or her with a token gift of earplugs.

Background/Applications

This game is really a variation of a morphological analysis, which is also known as the checkerboard approach. It helps participants systematically study a problem from new angles. Two variables are considered—benefits and people impacted, in this example. Each variable is broken down into sub-variables. Then each sub-variable from one list is juxtaposed with each sub-variable of the second list in an effort to bring some new possibilities to the problem or situation.

New shapes and configurations result—hence the term "morphological." Although the approach doesn't force participants to commit to any one course of action, it helps them examine possibilities they might overlook without juxtaposing variables, systematically, much like the squares on a checkerboard.

The prospective changes raise other issues, of course, which participants can then deal with in the meeting or at a later time. These are just some of the considerations to be covered in reference to the changes that might be caused by the group's decision:

- The changes will have to be communicated carefully and thoroughly to those who'll be impacted by them. Decisions will have to be made regarding *how* the communication will be done and *who* will do the communicating.

- Some attention will have to be paid to the willingness of those who'll be impacted to accept the change and not attempt to thwart it. Above all, benefits will have to be specified.

- A review must be conducted of the forces—technological, organization, external—that will help implement the change and those that will impede it.

- The decision-implementers and/or change-managers will need to find ways to melt down the existing roles, relationships, habits, and dependencies that made the existing operating procedure work. Not until this has been done should the change agents even consider making the new decision institutional.

68. Drawing a Decision Tree

TREED BY DECISIONS?

In a Nutshell

With this interactive game, participants add their thoughts to the branches of a simply drawn tree. Afterwards, they compare, discuss, and select the best of the choices.

Time

7 minutes.

What You'll Need

Four pieces of flip chart paper, taped together on a wall to form a square; marking pens, some with large points and some with finer points. (If possible, the fine-point markers should be dark colors.)

What to Do

1. In advance of the meeting, draw a simple, large tree outline on the chart-paper square. In the trunk of the tree, state the problem on which the group has been working. On each of the major branches, write one of the solutions the group has been discussing.

2. Distribute fine-point marking pens to the group. Ask them

to cluster around the tree. Give them three minutes to write the probable consequences of the various solutions in the form of smaller branches. (It's possible that a set of smaller branches will be required, to list the consequences of the consequences.)

3. Take three minutes to compare and discuss the alternatives.

4. Then, ask the participant who has worked the longest in the organization to write his or her choice of a solution on a sheet of paper and to fold it and place it in the center of the table.

5. In the final minute, ask the group to vote on the choices orally or with a show of hands.

6. If the group's vote differs from the choice written by the veteran employee, ask him or her why he or she made that choice. Also ask if he or she is willing to accept the group decision.

Background/Applications

We sometimes forget how many-layered most decisions are. Seldom can we choose a course of action and regard that choice as a simple event occurring in isolation. Instead, built around the decision is a whole infrastructure of experiences, values, mini-dramas, significant events, impressive personalities, external concerns, etc.

In a crisis situation, decision-makers don't have the luxury of time to deliberate and carefully analyze. They must react quickly, before the situation becomes even more critical. Meeting participants, fortunately, needn't deal with such exigencies. They have time to make decision trees, time to explore conditions from numerous perspectives in order to arrive at the best conclusion.

In *The Effective Executive*, Peter Drucker explores the nature of generic decisions, as compared with unique decisions.

With situations that are not novel, there will be rules, guide-lines, precedents, and/or boundaries to help decision-mak-ers. If the situation has never occurred before, then informa-tion has to be gathered. Drucker recommends, though, that before decision-makers gather information they gather opin-ions—opinions that are later tested by facts.

Finally, meeting leaders need to assure participants that the decision they are about to make is not a choice between right and wrong. (That would make the decision easy!) Rather, the decision is a choice among competing alternatives.

69. Using the Delphi Technique

A GREECE CAPRICE FOR AVOIDING GROUPTHINK

In a Nutshell

This ancient technique evolved in the Greek city of Delphi thousands of years ago. It's still used today because it can uncover true feelings about a decision to be made without exposing any one meeting participant to censure or scorn. Basically, participants write down their honest thoughts about the decision to be made. The meeting leader then reads the comments and re-opens the discussion—almost always with the advantage of new ideas to consider. This discussion is a vital preliminary step to decision-making, for it ensures the decision-makers are well informed on both sides of the issue.

Time

5-10 minutes.

What You'll Need

Flip chart and marking pens; participants will need paper and pens.

What to Do

1. Restate the issue by writing it on the flip chart.

2. Explain the value of the game. Sometimes meeting participants "go along with the crowd" because they hesitate to voice their opinions, for a number of reasons. Such hesitancy often leads to *groupthink*. This game, by calling for anonymous but honest feedback, goes a long way toward putting opinions on the table for the group to consider before voting.

3. Distribute a sheet of paper to each participant and ask them to write down what they're truly feeling about the issue on the flip chart. Ask them to be as objective and as honest as possible.

4. Read the comments and record on the flip chart any that have not been heard before.

5. Discuss these before moving on to a vote.

Background/Applications

The term "Abilene Paradox" has become synonymous with the dangers of groupthink. Jerry Harvey, in *The Abilene Paradox and Other Meditations on Management,* relates an incident that occurred in his family. Four people in Texas were sitting around on a hot afternoon and one of them suggested driving some 50 miles to Abilene for lunch. It turned out that each person had reservations about the comfort level—the car had no air conditioning—but no one questioned the idea. The four made an uncomfortable trip and had a mediocre lunch—even though no one really wanted to do it. The operative force here was niceness: everyone was too courteous to be the "wet blanket" that would smother the idea.

As nice as niceness may be, it can impede effective decision-making. If members of a meeting group are getting along *too* well or if they're too anxious to end the meeting, they can agree to something not because of its merits but because they want to expedite the process or they're unwilling to voice a dissenting opinion.

Historically, the worst example of groupthink may well be the decision to proceed with the Challenger launch. So great was the excitement, so extensive was the bonhomie surrounding the event that concerns about the O-rings were ignored.

Conflict in meetings is not necessarily a bad thing. It can help keep highly cohesive teams from rushing to judgments. Just as Tom Peters encourages organizations to treasure the "weirdos" on staff, meeting leaders should encourage devil's advocates to express their thoughts at meetings. Failure to do so could have dire consequences, for the group at the very least and perhaps for the organization.

70. Using the Nominal Group Technique

NOMINATE YOUR IDEA

In a Nutshell

In this game each participant has the opportunity to give input regarding a possible solution to the problem the group is dealing with. The team leader records the ideas, which are later clarified. Then each person selects his or her top five priorities. A simple tally determines the group decision: the item with the highest number (priority times number of votes) is the final group choice.

Time

7 minutes.

What You'll Need

3 x 5 cards; flip chart and marking pens; participants will need paper and pens.

What to Do

1. Write the problem the group has been dealing with as a full sentence on the flip chart. Ask participants to write it on their own papers as well.

2. Ask a volunteer to share his or her idea regarding a possible solution. Write it on the flip chart and then ask who has a similar idea. Add this to the flip chart list.

3. Continue asking each person to share their ideas but assure them they can pass if they choose to. The round-robin sharing continues as long as participants have something to say.

4. At this point there's no analysis or questioning regarding the list entries.

5. When the list is complete, label each item with a letter of the alphabet.

6. Spend a minute or two to clarify any entries, if necessary. Make certain the meaning of all listed items is clear.

7. Give each person five 3 x 5 cards. Working alone, participants choose the five items that represent their top priorities—one idea (or alphabet letter) on each card, along with a number that reflects the value they're giving each choice: "5" designates the top priority and "1" the least-favored choice.

8. Collect the cards and display the rankings. Multiply the rankings by the number of times each rank was voted for. (For example, Choice "A" might have had two votes for a 5 priority [= 10], one vote for a 4 priority [= 4], no votes for a 3 priority [= 0], four votes for a 2 priority [= 8], and two votes for a 1 priority [= 2]. The total for Choice "A" would be 24.)

Background/Applications

As long as group members have agreed to abide by the outcome, the item with the highest score becomes the group's decision. If there's no such agreement prior to the vote, the group will have to engage in further discussion and voting. In virtually every case, it's better to obtain that up-front agreement, if possible, so the group can commit to the outcome. Without such commitment, the nominal group technique can easily become a waste of time.

If the group has explored the risks beforehand, members may be more willing to commit to the outcome. In the risk analysis, you can help others examine the upside and downside of the decision. If there are high upside and low downside factors in the decision equation, it's easier to commit to the results of a numeric vote.

The nominal group technique works, but only when it's allowed to work. This means *you* will have to work to convince participants to abide by the outcome. Express your preference for deliberate action—not for deferring or delaying action.

71. Conducting a System Analysis

IF A PLAN

In a Nutshell

Decision-making is made easier when participants have had a chance to explore a problem through both qualitative and quantitative lenses. This micro version of a system analysis, IF A Plan, focuses on **i**mpressions, **f**acts, **a**nalysis, and a **p**lan. Participants share their impressions of the problem, record the facts, analyze both, and plan accordingly.

Time

5 minutes.

What You'll Need

Flip chart and marking pens; masking tape.

What to Do

1. Begin by writing the problem on the flip chart.

2. For a minute or so, invite participants to share their qualitative views of the problem: their impressions, intuition, opinions, feelings, worries, etc. Record their input.

3. Next, spend a minute asking for and listing factual data—

statistics, test results, facts, figures, empirical data, research studies, poll, survey results, etc. Record these as well.

4. Spend two minutes studying information listed—both subjective and objective. Try to develop a big-picture or system analysis.

5. Spend the last three minutes working out a plan. Identify options available and decide on one that's most viable, given the discussion.

Background/Applications

The consideration of subjective and objective, qualitative and quantitative, analytical and anecdotal is espoused by numerous authorities, not the least of whom is Spencer Johnson. In *Yes or No: The Guide to Better Decisions,* he speaks of decisions that come from both the head and the heart. And, he encourages asking correlative questions from both categories.

Like many others, he advises decision-makers to keep the consequences in mind. One such consequence could be a decision so successful in its implementation that it causes unanticipated problems, greater than the original problem. On the other hand, sometimes a decision is so unsuccessful in its implementation that it causes even greater difficulties.

Perhaps the best example of the latter comes from Australia, which faced a problem of sugar cane beetles in the 1930s. To save the crops, scientists introduced giant marine toads native to Central and South America. Unfortunately, those highly poisonous toads not only failed to control the beetles, but quickly multiplied and became a menace to the delicate ecosystem unprepared for their numbers.

Careful analysis—of both impressions and facts—might have prevented implementing this "solution" that failed and caused greater problems. But in your meetings, you can apply analyses like IF A Plan to help improve the decision-making process.

72. Employing Comparative Valuation

A POWerful Analysis

In a Nutshell

The process of comparative analysis is lengthy, but you can employ a miniature version of it, based on three criteria that form the mnemonic POW, as in *power*ful. The group compiles a list of choices. The participants then vote on their favorite or most **p**opular. Next, they rate the choices twice, according to two criteria: in terms of being least **o**perative or least optimized at present and in terms of having the highest value or **w**orth. Finally, by a show of hands, you can tally the votes. Participants are often interested to see that the choice that's most popular initially is not the one that ends up on top.

Time

5 minutes.

What You'll Need

Flip chart and marking pens; participants will need paper and pens.

What to Do

1. Begin with a list of brainstormed choices—10 is a good number—on the flip chart. Have three columns next to the list—one labeled "P," the second labeled "O," and the third labeled "W."

2. Ask participants to take a minute and to write down the choice that is their favorite at this point—the choice that they feel is the best decision for the group to make. Record their choices by writing the "P" in the first column beside each participant's favorite choice.

3. Next, ask participants to think about the choices and rate them 1-10, giving the highest rating to the choice that's *least optimized* at present. Poll the participants and record the scores in the "O" column. (For example, assume the group is meeting about the problem of low workplace morale. One of the choices is "Attend a stress class." If the classes are already being offered, the optimization score would be quite low—a 1 or 2. Another choice is "Show inspirational videos at lunchtime." If the organization has never done this, the optimization score would be a 9 or 10, meaning there's high potential use.)

4. Finally, have the participants rate the choices 1-10 according to *value* or *worth*: "How good is the idea?" The greater the worth, the higher the rating. Poll the participants and write the number in the "W" column.

5. For the remaining minute, look over the items and the numbers in the middle and last columns. The most beneficial course of action is the one with very high O and W scores: it has a very high worth but is currently not being optimized. (If the organization already has a similar plan under way, it's futile to make plans to reinstitute it.) Once you've determined the choice that's best in terms of low optimization and high worth, compare it with the initial, most popular choice. It's usually not the same.

Background/Applications

The full comparative valuation process takes considerably more than seven minutes but is warranted when the choices concern strategic planning, for example.

It begins with a brainstormed list of 20-30 possibilities. The list is narrowed to 10. Then, each choice is compared with each of the others: Which do I like more? Which do I think has a slight edge over the other? The better choice is recorded.

Choice #1 is compared with Choice #2 and #1 or #2 is listed. Then, Choice #1 is compared with Choice #3 and #1 or #3 is listed. This process continues until #1 has been compared with each of the other nine possibilities. Then, the same process is used for Choice #2 (comparing with Choices #3 through #10), for Choice #3 (comparing with Choices #4 through #10), and so on, until Choice #9 is compared with Choice #10. There will be a total of 45 "answers" to all these comparisons.

	1	2	3	4	5	6	7	8	9	10
1		1	3	1	1	6	7	1	1	1
2			3	2	5	2	2	8	2	10
3				3	5	6	3	3	9	3
4					5	6	4	8	9	4
5						5	7	5	5	10
6							7	6	9	6
7								7	9	10
8									9	10
9										10
10										

This process works both for an individual with a critical choice to make and for a group. (If you're working with a team, you'll calculate group averages.)

First, the participants indicate their choices for popularity. Save these votes until the end, so you can 1) show that the popular choice is usually not the best choice and 2) use them as a tie-breaker if there are two final options of nearly equal merit.

Then, you'll determine the percentage of satisfaction (1 = low; 100 = high) concerning the 10 choices and the degree to which their potential is being utilized. If an option listed among the 10 choices is already in place but is not working well, you'd assign it a low percentage. If the option is not being used at all or is being used in only one area but you think it could be used throughout the organization, you'd again have to assign a low percentage, because the choice is not being optimized. On the other hand, if an option is already successful and widely used, the score might be 90% or 100%, indicating that the organization is making the best possible use of this option's potential. Calculate group averages of these scores.

Next, assign a number from 1 (low) to 10 (high) to reflect the value or merit of the options. Average the group scores.

Finally, plot the percentage numbers and the worth numbers on a grid, with the following four quadrants:

- Low Optimization, Low Worth

- Low Optimization, High Worth

- High Optimization, Low Worth

- High Optimization, High Worth

Your team will be tempted to select items in the High Optimization, High Worth quadrant as the ones to pursue. This is faulty thinking, though, because High Optimization means your efforts would be repetitive. Choosing an item

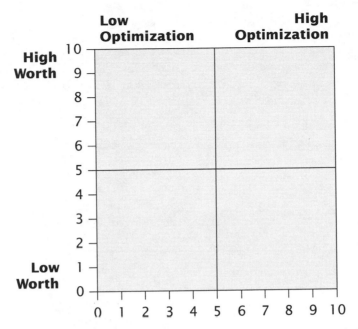

with High Worth but Low Optimization is bound to produce better results on your investment of resources.

If time permits, consider how and why the decision was reached. For example, compare individual responses with the group response. If there are radical differences, the group members should ask, "Do I know something the others don't know?" or "Do others know something I don't know?" The analysis can yield some important insights.

Part Nine

MAKING SURE MEETINGS END ON TIME

Numerous factors go into the equation for successful meeting closure. Among them are the need to offer a final opportunity for quieter participants to share their thoughts, the opportunity for participants to give feedback to the meeting leader, and the opportunity for the meeting leader to involve participants in the closure activities of summarizing what's been done, confirming understandings reached, affirming the commitment to the meeting goal, and reviewing assignments for the next meeting.

For some meetings, the closure motto seems to be "We'll meet forever or until meeting participants develop laryngitis—whichever comes first!" If you've ever participated in such a meeting, you'll appreciate the first game in this section, "Ensuring Equal Participation." It gives everyone at the meeting a chance to burst the dominant speaker's talk balloon, quite literally.

The second game permits participants to give feedback, in a humorous fashion, to the meeting leader directly, particularly if he or she tends to run over at the end of meetings. The final game is a gift—the gift of closure that participants can give to each other.

All too often, closure is rushed. Participants begin looking at their watches and the reality of what awaits them back in the office begins to intrude. To ensure the proper wrap-up, meeting leaders have to plan in advance. But ... if the plan goes awry, these three games will help the meeting end back on track.

73. *Ensuring Equal Participation*

BALLOON BURSTS

In a Nutshell

Often, near the end of a meeting, participants feel compelled to share their final thoughts in a last-ditch effort to make their opinions prevail. This game is a fun way to ensure that participants keep their final comments to a minimum so the meeting can end on time. Any participant who feels that another is talking on to excess can burst a balloon and stop the hot air. The "pop" will not only startle participants into laughter (and perhaps out of slumber), but also serve as a funny reminder to the verbose member that it's time to *wind* down (pronounced as both a noun and a verb).

Time

5 seconds.

What You'll Need

For every participant, a blown-up balloon attached to a string, tied or taped to the right leg of every participant's chair, and a closed safety pin, placed on each participant's seat—both before anyone arrives.

What to Do

1. Commend the group for their commitment (if the game is used at beginning of the meeting) or their accomplishment (if the game is used near the end of the meeting). Say that you're determined to keep the meeting on track up to the last moment so you can adjourn on time.

2. Explain that each person will find a balloon attached to his or her chair and a pin nearby for immediate use, if necessary. Instruct participants to pop the balloon at any point when any participant (or the leader) goes on talking too long.

3. Should the eventuality occur, thank the talker (once the laughter and surprise have died down) for being willing to accede to the group's wishes.

Background/Applications

The balloon burst serves two encoding purposes: it startles participants out of the meeting-end stupor that often occurs at this time and it reminds participants of the need to get to the point so the meeting can get to the end.

Although the meeting leader is responsible for directing the final minutes and the final words of the meeting toward a meaningful conclusion, this game affords participants a participatory role. They can have a direct hand in reminding each other of the need to be succinct.

A bit of drama helps people remember information. The anticipation of a balloon burst and the impact of the surprise are likely to make the meeting more memorable. Of course, when the prolix participant has been interrupted and humorously silenced, the meeting leader has to step in to separate the verbal wheat from the chaff of prolixity, to remind participants of the relevant ideas, to thank the speaker, perhaps, for the ideas he or she has shared, and to transition from the interrupted monolog to the work at hand.

74. Sharing Feedback with the Meeting Leader

HAMMING IT DOWN

In a Nutshell

The purpose of this silent, visual game is to offer the meeting leader feedback regarding his or her verbosity. To help the talkative leader spend less time "hamming it up" in the spotlight, participants will place a picture of a ham in the center of the meeting table whenever the leader's back is turned.

Time

10 seconds.

What You'll Need

Pictures of hams (cut out from mail-order catalogs of edible gifts or sketched), glued to 6 x 8 cards.

What to Do

1. Distribute a picture of a ham to each participant.

2. Ask them to move the ham pictures to the center of the table if you should ever spend too much time being

histrionic or sharing your own experiences.

3. Remember to turn your back to the group from time to time during the meeting—such as to write on the flip chart, to walk around the room, or to bend down to tie your shoe.

4. If you should find one or more ham pictures at the center of the table, laugh to show your appreciation of their efforts to keep you on track and then do your best to stay on track for the remainder of the meeting.

Background/Applications

Most meeting leaders find it difficult or at least unnatural to not hold the starring role, to remain in the background. At the heart of the difficulty is that the leader or facilitator generally has that role because of his or her extensive experience. Ironically, it's often that very experience that causes the meeting leader to intervene at times and in places where restraint should be used. Meeting leaders need to exercise patience, permitting participants to come to insights that the leader could easily have provided. Questions help expedite the process of arriving at insights.

At the heart of this game is a good-natured invitation to silence the leader who controls rather than facilitates. The leader must not take offense, of course, but must act on the reactions of participants by quickly and smoothly getting back to a secondary role and yet moving the meeting to an efficient conclusion. (The braver among you will encourage participants to react to your role throughout the meeting, not just at the end.)

75. Involving Participants with Closure

UNWRAP YOUR WRAP-UP

In a Nutshell

This final game gives participants a chance to have the final word. Each person unwraps a gift box that contains a request for him or her to give a one-sentence wrap-up. You'll conclude with an expression of gratitude for their time and admiration for their collective accomplishment.

Time

5-10 minutes.

What You'll Need

One small, nicely wrapped box for each participant. Inside each box, have one of these five requests:

- *Please make a one-sentence statement about the group's dedication.*

- *Please make a one-sentence statement about what you've learned in this meeting.*

- *Please make a one-sentence statement concerning what you've most enjoyed about this meeting and the participants.*

- *Please make a one-sentence statement telling how the organization might benefit from what was done in this meeting.*

- *Please make a one-sentence statement about the future.*

What to Do

1. Five minutes before the meeting is scheduled to end (planning on one additional minute if there are more than five participants), announce that you have a small gift for each participant but—unable as you are to escape from your role as meeting leader—the gift is actually a final request.

2. Distribute the gifts and ask participants to unwrap their gifts and make their statements.

3. Bring closure by thanking the participants for what they've accomplished and mention how their efforts will be applied in the future.

Background/Applications

Ideally, the maintenance tasks—such as praising, listening, socializing, showing concern, motivating, etc.—have been managed throughout the meeting, by both the meeting leader and the participants. This game represents a final opportunity for concentrating on the social glue that keeps participants bound to one another and, ultimately, to the mission.

An alternative to this game has each participant write a wrap-up comment, place it in a box, quickly wrap the box, and present it to another person to unwrap and read. Participants can also place the gifts in the center of the table and then take another gift from the pile, to unwrap and read. (Of course, the leader could take over the closure responsibility entirely and still give a gift box with a personalized message of appreciation to each participant.)

About the Author

Dr. Marlene Caroselli, author of 51 business books (see http://hometown.aol.com/mccpd and Amazon.com) is an international keynote speaker and corporate trainer for *Fortune* 100 companies, government agencies, educational institutions, and professional organizations. She contributes frequently to a number of well-known publications (among them Stephen Covey's Excellence publications and Lakewood Publications). Her first book, *The Language of Leadership*, was chosen a main selection by Newbridge's Executive Development Book Club. A more recent book, *Principled Persuasion*, was just named a Director's Choice by Doubleday Book Club.